TIBETAN ZEN

Tibetan Zen

Discovering a Lost Tradition

Sam van Schaik

SNOW LION
BOSTON & LONDON
2015

Snow Lion
An imprint of Shambhala Publications, Inc.
Horticultural Hall
300 Massachusetts Avenue
Boston, Massachusetts 02115
www.shambhala.com

9 8 7 6 5 4 3 2 1

First Edition
Printed in the United States of America

♾ This edition is printed on acid-free paper that meets the
American National Standards Institute z39.48 Standard.
♻ Shambhala makes every effort to print on recycled paper.
For more information please visit www.shambhala.com.

Distributed in the United States by Penguin Random House LLC
and in Canada by Random House of Canada Ltd

Designed by Gopa and Ted 2, Inc.

Library of Congress Cataloging-in-Publication Data

Van Schaik, Sam, author.
Tibetan Zen: discovering a lost tradition / Sam van Schaik.
—First edition.
pages cm
ISBN 978-1-55939-446-8 (paperback: alk. paper)
1. Zen Buddhism—Tibet Region—Doctrines—History. 2. Zen
literature—China—Dunhuang Caves—Translations into English.
I. Title.
BQ9262.9.T53V36 2015
294.3'92709515—dc23
2014042693

To Ananda

Contents

Acknowledgments

This book has its beginning in work that I did with Jacob Dalton on the Tibetan Dunhuang manuscripts during the years 2002 to 2005. In the years that followed, I was able to spend time with John McRae and other Sinologists, from whom I learned much about Chinese Zen, or Chan. In 2010 I was awarded a three-year grant by the British Academy to study and translate the Tibetan Zen manuscripts. During this project I had the privilege of working with Drikung Kyabgön Chetsang Rinpoche to create online editions of all the Tibetan Zen texts, now available at the website of the International Dunhuang Project. I have been lucky to work with many great colleagues at the British Library and would especially like to thank Burkhard Quessel and Susan Whitfield for their support. My erstwhile colleague Imre Galambos has always been willing to answer my questions about Chinese sources. Finally I'd like to thank Nikko Odiseos of Shambhala Publications for his interest in this book, and Michael Wakoff for his sympathetic copyediting.

Abbreviations

BD	Dunhuang manuscripts in the National Library of China
D	The Derge edition of the *bka' 'gyur* and *bstan 'gyur*
IOL Tib J	Tibetan Dunhuang manuscripts in the British Library
Or.8210	Chinese Dunhuang manuscripts in the British Library
Or.15000	Tibetan manuscripts from Central Asian sites in the British Library
Pelliot chinois	Chinese Dunhuang manuscripts in the Bibliothèque nationale de France
Pelliot tibétain	Tibetan Dunhuang manuscripts in the Bibliothèque nationale de France
T	*Taisho Tripiṭaka:* the Chinese Buddhist canon

When references are given to manuscripts, *r* refers to the recto (front) and *v* refers to the verso (back). The method of numbering depends on the format. Pothi folios are numbered 1r, 1v, 2r, 2v, and so on. Concertina folios are numbered r1, r2, r3, and so on, until one reaches the verso, where the manuscript is flipped over and continues as v1, v2, v3, and so on. Scrolls in vertical format are numbered simply as r or v followed by line numbers, while those in horizontal format are numbered r1 for the first column of text, r2 for the second, and so on (and v1, v2, and so forth, on the verso).

TIBETAN ZEN

Introduction

A LOST TRADITION?

Censured in Tibet, forgotten in China, the Tibetan version of Zen was almost completely lost. Zen first came to Tibet in the eighth century, when Chinese teachers were invited there at the height of the Tibetan empire. According to traditional histories, doctrinal disagreements developed between Indian and Chinese Buddhists at the Tibetan court, and the Tibetan emperor called for the situation to be resolved in a formal debate. When the debate resulted in a decisive win by the Indian side, the Zen teachers were sent back to China. Though this story has been questioned, it is clear that the popularity of Zen declined in Tibet, and its original texts were all but forgotten.

This changed at the beginning of the twentieth century with the discovery of a sealed cave full of ancient manuscripts in Dunhuang in Chinese Central Asia. The Tibetan manuscripts from the cave have been dated to the ninth and tenth centuries, making them the earliest known source materials for Tibetan Buddhism. Among them are some fifty manuscripts containing the only surviving original Tibetan Zen texts, the primary source material for understanding Tibetan Zen. Since the manuscripts offer a snapshot of the early Zen tradition in the eighth to tenth centuries, they are significant sources for the study of Chinese, Japanese, and Korean Zen as well. Furthermore, Tibetan Zen appears to have developed into a distinct tradition, incorporating elements of tantric Buddhism, and this fascinating synthesis remains little understood.[1]

The sealed cave at Dunhuang was part of a complex of Buddhist cave shrines, cut into a cliff at the edge of the Central Asian desert. We know tantalizingly little about the cave: neither why it was filled with manuscripts nor why it was sealed. But we have the results of this accident of history, in the thousands of books in Chinese, Tibetan, Turkic, Sanskrit, and other languages, along with Buddhist paintings and temple banners. In fact, the term "library cave" is misleading, for if one thing is clear, it is that this cache of manuscripts does not form any kind of coherent library collection. Alongside Buddhist scriptures and treatises are notebooks, shopping lists, writing exercises, letters, contracts, sketches, and scurrilous off-the-cuff verses.

So rather than the orderly and carefully selected contents of a library, what was put into the cave was a jumble of material from the everyday life of this town and its monasteries. For many scholars who have studied texts from the cave over the past century, this has seemed an obstacle, but for our project of understanding a once-living tradition that since died out, it is an advantage. In the Tibetan tradition, we already have a Buddhist canon containing over one hundred volumes of scriptures, commentaries, and treatises. Yet a canon does not represent the day-to-day practice of a religious tradition. It is mediated by the decisions of editors and patrons, which may have more to do with the politics of canonization—by which a tradition defines itself—than with everyday religious life. In a canon, texts are grouped into rubrics alongside similar texts, and these rubrics stratify texts that are, outside of the canon, much more mixed up and heterogenous.

This is the advantage of the cache of manuscripts from the cave in Dunhuang. They might be "sacred waste"—as the first European to visit the caves, Aurel Stein, referred to them—but they have not been carefully selected and ordered to present an idealized image of a tradition, as canonical collections are. In this disorderly jumble, texts rub up against each other in a way that would never be allowed in the cold piety of the canon. We can ask, and perhaps answer, the questions: what did people do with these texts; what they were they used for?

Let's take an example: the earliest surviving Tibetan Zen manuscript. This is a scroll fragment found not in Dunhuang but in the ruins of a Tibetan fort farther to the west. This fort, now known by its Turkic name, Miran, was built and used by the Tibetans to guard the border of their empire from the mid-eighth to mid-ninth centuries. The traditional textual approach to this unique object would be to transcribe the Zen text, append the place where it was found and the range of dates in between which it might have been written, and then proceed in the realm of pure textuality, with comparisons to other similarly context-free texts.

Rather than rushing to leave the fort, text in hand, we can stay for a little longer and look at some of the other objects that were found there alongside this scroll by the archaeologist Aurel Stein. There are a soldier's things: leather scales from armor, an arrowhead, and a feathered arrow shaft. There are things that anyone might have used: leather pouches, a comb, a key, a wooden-handled knife, a six-sided die. Then there are things used in the production of manuscripts: a split-nibbed pen and three seals with horn handles, used to stamp official letters and contracts. These were the companions of the earliest Tibetan Zen text for over a thousand years, and we should not be too quick to separate them.

As for the other manuscripts from the fort, most of them are official communiqués between different outposts of the Tibetan empire. The shorter day-to-day messages were sent on strips of wood, sometimes on two pieces that could be bound together with string and sealed with clay. When supplies were requested, the wood slip was marked and the bottom right corner cut off, as a chit that could be compared with the original order when the supplies arrived. What unites the objects found in the fort with these official documents is that we tend to approach them by trying to work out what people used them for. What were the patterns of behavior behind these objects? Was the die used for divination, or gambling, or both? How often did the soldier have to use those arrows? And did he also use the pen to dash off quick messages, or was there a trained scribe in the fort? Once they were written, who took them to the nearest military headquarters, and who brought back food and other supplies? Though it might not always be possible to answer these questions, the asking of them seems obvious, and sensible.

So, what if we were to ask the same questions about the Zen text from Miran (or rather, the manuscript from which the text has been abstracted) as we want to ask about the die, the arrows, and the leather pouch. We would ask: How was it made? Who brought it here? Who used it, and for what purposes? And as they do for archaeologists, these questions would become questions about wider patterns of behavior. By taking a range of objects from a complex of sites and placing them in relation to each other, we may be able to discern these patterns. This would allow us to consider not just the meaning of the text but its use, the practice in which it was embedded.

The Tibetan Zen scroll was brought to Miran, for there were no papermaking facilities there, for some purpose. Of course, we may never discern that purpose, but by paying close attention to the manuscript, we might find a few clues. For example, turning it over, we find another text written on the verso, in slightly scruffier writing than the Zen text. This is a tantric text, an explanation of the practice of making offerings to Buddhist deities in order to accomplish the four activities of pacifying, increasing, magnetizing, and subjugating: practices that could well be of interest to soldiers in a remote fort. So the Tibetan Zen text could just have come along for the ride, rather than being brought to be practiced. On other hand, it might also have been part of a practice, brought by a lay or monastic Buddhist. But can we really get from objects like this to the everyday practices of which they were a part?

MANUSCRIPTS AND PRACTICES

Approaching the Tibetan Zen manuscripts as active participants in everyday social practices does not just mean looking for texts that describe social practices. It means seeing all texts as practices, in their embodied nature as physical manuscripts. To show how this might work, let us look at the most important and most widely studied of the Tibetan Zen manuscripts, Pelliot tibétain 116, a compendium of ten different texts.

This is a big and beautifully written manuscript, folded in the concertina format into 124 panels, each seven by thirty centimeters, and filled with four lines of text. With a concertina manuscript, you read with two panels facing you, and turn them over as you go; when you reach the end, you turn the whole thing over and start reading the back of the manuscript in the same way. The construction of a concertina of over one hundred panels required many sheets of paper, and a combination of folding, gluing, and stitching. It became popular in the mid-ninth century and seems to have been particularly favored by the Tibetan speakers at Dunhuang: there are around 260 of them in the British and French collections, and 90 percent are written in Tibetan.

The first and second texts of Pelliot tibétain 116 are not Zen texts per se. They are Buddhist texts whose popularity spans most traditions: the *Prayer of Excellent Conduct* and the *Vajracchedikā sūtra*. Presumably because of the ubiquity of these two texts, the reproduction of the manuscript, which formed the basis for most studies of it, simply omitted the first 107 panels. The first two texts, the reason for their inclusion, and their laborious copying by a scribe were simply removed from consideration.

In the textual approach, even the most immediate context, the proximity of other texts to the text in question, can be forgotten once the text is extracted. Thus most studies of Pelliot tibétain 116 have focused on one of its ten texts, with little or no reference to any of the others, and certainly not to the two "non-Zen" texts at the beginning of the manuscript. In fact, these two texts are vital to understanding the manuscript, for they offer us a suggestion about why it was made and how it was used. The presence of the *Prayer of Excellent Conduct* at the beginning of the manuscript indicates that it was made to facilitate the performance of a ritual, the ceremony of taking the precepts of a bodhisattva. This is a series of vows found only in the Buddhism of the greater vehicle (*mahāyāna*) and directed to the aspiration of the bodhisattva: to strive for the enlightenment of all sentient beings. The bodhisattva precepts ceremony originated in India but became especially popular in China, where mass precepts ceremonies were held on specially constructed platforms.

These bodhisattva precepts ceremonies complemented the ceremonies of conferring the monastic *prātimokṣa* vows. The bodhisattva precepts could be taken by lay people as well as already-ordained monks and nuns. Furthermore, the precepts had the advantage over the monastic ordination of needing only a single master to confer them. This made it possible for charismatic masters like Reverend Kim and Shenhui to use the precepts platform to teach and to lead group meditation practice.

The popularity of these precepts ceremonies coincided with the emergence of self-conscious Zen lineages during the eighth century, so that, as Wendi Adamek has put it, "Chan can be said to have been born on the bodhisattva precepts platform."[2] The ceremony of receiving the precepts of the bodhisattva took place in the context of a Zen lineage and was expanded to include an introduction to the Zen style of meditation.

The importance of the platform ceremony in Zen lineages is also evident among the Dunhuang manuscripts. For example, one of the most popular early Zen texts, the *Platform Sutra* (which is found in several versions among the Dunhuang manuscripts), is constructed around an ordination sermon by the sixth patriarch Huineng. Another platform sermon by Huineng's disciple Shenhui is also found in the Dunhuang manuscripts.

How does the arrangement of the texts in Pelliot tibétain 116 suggest the context of a precepts ceremony? The *Prayer of Excellent Conduct* is an aspirational text written in the first person, expressing the aim of bringing about the welfare and enlightenment of all beings. This is the aspiration of the bodhisattva, which is formalized in Buddhist praxis by the ceremony of taking the bodhisattva precepts. The presence of the *Prayer of Excellent Conduct* at the beginning of the compendium is the first clue that the manuscript may have been made for use in such ceremonies. The prayer is followed by the *Vajracchedikā* (better known in English as the *Diamond Sutra*), one of the most popular expositions of the concept of emptiness, which states that all things are interdependent, and thus nothing can have an intrinsic essence. In this scriptural text, the Buddha repeatedly makes contradictory statements, celebrating the virtuous path of a bodhisattva and the qualities of a buddha at the same time as denying that that they exist. This approach is a challenge to dualistic concepts of self and other, existence and nonexistence, and the like. This use of deliberate paradox as a teaching method had a strong influence on the development of the Zen tradition.

The *Vajracchedikā* also occupies a central place in the *Platform Sutra,* which begins with the story of how Huineng became the sixth patriarch of the lineage. Huineng is said to have left home and gone in search of the fifth patriarch after hearing the *Vajracchedikā* being recited in the marketplace. Later in the narrative, the fifth patriarch transmits his authority and wisdom to Huineng by explaining the *Vajracchedikā* to him. After this biographical sketch, the *Platform Sutra* turns into a sermon given by Huineng in a ceremony of bestowing precepts. This ceremony begins with taking refuge in the Buddha, his teachings, and the community of monks and lay practitioners. Then follows the vow of the bodhisattva and an exposition of the meaning of emptiness, with particular reference, again, to the *Vajracchedikā*.

Thus the first and second texts in Pelliot tibétain 116 mirror the themes of ordination sermons like the one we find in the *Platform Sutra*: bestowing the precepts of the bodhisattva and expounding emptiness. And they continue to follow the same path as we read the other texts in Pelliot tibétain 116—an introduction to the basic theme of Zen Buddhism, the immanence of the enlightened state in the ordinary person, followed by instructions on meditation, and ending with an inspiring song. This ceremony would be the central ritual of an event that was often planned well in advance, giving monastics and lay people time to travel to the site of the ceremony, and could last over several days or weeks, the transmission of the precepts being followed by a meditation retreat.[3]

A look at the other texts in Pelliot tibétain 116, and indeed its great length, suggests that it was perhaps not merely read from beginning to end. Several of the texts in this compendium are themselves anthologies of paraphrases from Zen teachers and passages from scriptures. Others are written in a question and answer format from which individual passages can be easily extracted. The manuscript was probably used as a sourcebook for the ceremony, rather than a strict liturgy, just as catechisms and compendia of scriptural passages and paraphrases have been used in other contexts, in different forms of Buddhism as well as in other religious traditions.[4] Another close look at the manuscript gives a suggestive clue that this was the case—somebody has marked various points in the texts with a small cross, perhaps a visual reminder to make use of a particular passage.[5]

So, we can now suggest why somebody, or perhaps several people, took the time and expense to create this manuscript, why it became much worn by use, and why it was worth repairing again. It was created for a purpose; it had a function, and this function can tell us as much about the practice of Tibetan Zen as the contents of the texts. This shows the value of looking at manuscripts as things that play active roles in human practices. And, of course, the texts are a part of this approach, but if our reading of texts can happen without discarding the physical manuscript, we have the potential of a much richer understanding of the way the texts were used.

In the early phase of Western interest in Zen, it was thought to be opposed to any form of ritual observance. It is now generally accepted that this was a false picture informed by the Protestant sensibilities and antiestablishment politics of the era. In fact, as the editor of a recent volume on Zen ritual puts it, "Zen life is overwhelmingly a life of ritual."[6]

Of course, it is not so easy to evoke the ritual life of a tradition that no longer exists. While this book offers translations of Tibetan Zen manuscripts, I have also attempted to evoke, to some extent, the community in which they once played a part, and in so doing, get closer to a sense of the range of practices in which they functioned. Probably a word about the way I am using the term "ritual" is necessary here. The word is used to denote a variety of things, as many have noted. Here, I use the term to refer to a specific kind of practice: a group activity, performed self-consciously and in a conventional manner, in order to achieve an end. This use is analogous with "ceremony," and I use the two terms interchangeably.[7]

In the translations in this book, along with the ceremonies and daily recitation practices that we have already discussed, we will also look at the role of teaching and the receiving of teachings, of which the manuscripts also have much to tell us. And in this context, we will see how the legitimation of practice and the way it is positioned in a tradition are among the most important heuristic methods used by teachers. Through these manuscripts, I hope to communicate a sense of how an emerging tradition is propagated by teachers, strengthened and expanded through group rituals, internalized through meditation, supported by patrons, and defended against external threats.

ZEN IN CHINA

Modern scholarship is fairly united in the conclusion that there was no Zen "school" as such before the advent of the Song dynasty in the late tenth century. Rather, there were a variety of groups—generally composed of a single master and his disciples—teaching and practicing an approach that emphasized meditation (*dhyāna* or in Chinese, *chan*).[8] Therefore, if we are to talk about Zen or Chan before this time (and this includes Tibetan Zen), we should remember to consider it an umbrella term sheltering these various practices, brought together not by a shared essential trait but by a complex of family resemblances. These include but are not limited to instructions on how to meditate, teachings on the immanence of enlightenment in the mind, the ritual of bestowing the bodhisattva precepts, and allied with this, the transmission of lineages that in most but not all cases include the figure of Bodhidharma. However, the radical antinomianism and illogical dialogue associated with the later, full-fledged Chan tradition are not very evident in the Tibetan and Chinese lineages on which it was based.

Traditionally, the history of Chan in China is presented as an unbroken lineage, coming from a single source that can be traced back to Śākyamuni Buddha, brought to China by the Indian monk Bodhidharma, and then dividing, tree-like, into different schools. Modern scholarship has concluded that this is an idealized image, presenting the tradition as a lineage like a "string of pearls" rather than the heterogenous, distributed, and varied phenomenon that we see when we investigate early sources—in particular the Dunhuang manuscripts. An alternative picture of the historical development of Chan up to the fourteenth century has developed in the work of Japanese and American scholars in the twentieth century, largely based on the Dunhuang manuscripts. The following schema by John McRae (2003) is indicative:

Proto-Chan (ca. 500–600)
Early Chan (ca. 600–900)
Middle Chan (ca. 750–1000)
Song-Dynasty Chan (ca. 950–1300)

As McRae points out, it is a curious and not yet fully explained fact that the Dunhuang manuscripts provide no sources for Middle and Song-Dynasty Chan, despite being dated from as late as the early eleventh century. This shows at least that the success of the exponents of Middle Chan was limited to specific regions and in Dunhuang, Chan continued to develop with minimal influence from them and their followers. Thus in Dunhuang we are dealing with Early Chan, with Proto-Chan being evident only through its role in lineage accounts and in the practices of the Early Chan teachers. There are two plausible explanations for this: geographical and chronological. The geographical explanation is that movements that later became influential across the Chan tradition as whole began as local developments, like that of Mazu (709–88) and his followers, which began in Jiangxi in the southeast of China, about as far away from Dunhuang as could be. Until much later, these local lineages simply did not have an impact across the whole of the Chinese cultural sphere.

The second explanation is that such movements did not exist in the way that they are portrayed in later sources. Thus the "encounter dialogues" that came to typify Song-Dynasty Chan purport to represent the teachings and teaching styles of earlier masters, but may be misleading in this respect, as John McRae argues:

> What is being referred to is not some collection of activities and events that actually happened in the eighth through tenth centuries, but instead the retrospective re-creation of those activities and events, the imagined identities of the magical figures of the Tang, within the minds of Song-Dynasty Chan devotees.[9]

Thus, if Middle Chan is primarily a retrospective construct of Song-Dynasty Chan, we should not expect to find it in preeleventh-century sources. The Chan that we find at Dunhuang is not necessarily marginal; rather it is one of many local complexes of Chan practice, predating the emerging Chan orthodoxy of the eleventh century. In a context in which there is no "Chan school" and various versions of Chan lineages are found across China and Tibet, turning our attention to the local avoids anachronistic references to Chan as if it were a single entity.

A brief historical sketch of Early Chan begins with the figure of Bodhidharma, whose obscurity as a historical figure is matched by his vivid presence in the Chan lineage. During the sixth century, the followers of Bodhidharma and his Chinese student Huike promoted a text called *Treatise on the Two Entrances and Four Practices* that emphasized the enlightened nature present in the awareness of all living beings ("the entrance of the principle") and that also briefly described how to practice ("the entrance of practice"). Essentially, the text enjoins a form of practice that is without the concept of practice, so that "even when you are practicing the six perfections, you are not practicing anything."

In the following century, Chan lineage based on the teachings embodied in the *Treatise on the Two Entrances and Four Practices* flourished in rural locations such as the "East Mountain" at Huangmei. Writings from the East Mountain monks describe meditation practices in more detail, including the practice of "observing the mind."[10] At the very end of the seventh century, one of the heirs to the East Mountain lineage, a monk called Shenxiu (606?–706), was invited to the imperial capital by the Empress Wu Zeitian (r. 690–705), and this marks the beginning of the ascent of Chan to becoming the dominant force in Chinese Buddhism. Working in both of the imperial capital cities of Loyang and Chang'an, Shenxiu was an influential teacher and author, and many of his students were also influential figures.

As more opportunities developed for monks teaching from Chan lineages to gather students and wealthy patrons, Chan became both more widespread and more various. In the eighth century, new groups of Chan teachers and students sprang up in (modern) Sichuan province. The spread of Chan outside of the palaces and monasteries was effected through mass ceremonies of lay ordination, in which the vows of the bodhisattva (the greater vehicle aspiration to save all sentient beings) were conferred at the same time as the nature of one's own awareness as a fully enlightened buddha. These ordinations were performed on platforms and often included sermons by charismatic and radical teachers like Shenhui and Wuzhu. Shenhui used his sermons to directly criticize influential rivals like the students of Shenxiu, with a somewhat crude critique of meditation practice in all its forms. Wuzhu, on the other hand, eschewed all forms of religious activity apart from meditation practice. Thus, by the end of the eighth century, Chan teachings had spread across China, and indeed to Tibet, without yet having been shaped into a single consistent tradition as such.[11]

The Chan manuscripts from Dunhuang (Tibetan and Chinese) present an inclusive and evolving state of affairs during the ninth and tenth centuries, bringing together most of what had gone before. Bodhidharma is here as an important figure in the lineage of Chan teachers, but not necessarily the founding figure, and in one lineage, he does not appear at all. Nor is Bodhidharma always cited in collections of the teachings of Chan masters. These masters are mainly from the seventh and eighth centuries and include both those who are well known to the later tradition and many others who have disappeared into obscurity. Though the manuscripts are mainly from the ninth and tenth centuries, it is these seventh- and eighth-century teachers (or at least the later representation of them) who dominate; thus we seem to be seeing a Chan tradition in the process of defining itself through the image of these masters and the teachings attributed to them.

A key figure on the Dunhuang scene, in both Chinese and Tibetan sources, is the Chan master known as Moheyan. Teaching in the second half of the eighth century, he was part of the generation that followed Shenhui's polemical attacks on established Chan meditation practices. What remains of Moheyan's teachings are clearly attempts to marry practices taught by preceding generations with the antipractice rhetoric of Shenhui. Moheyan studied with Xiangmo Zang, one of the established teachers criticized by Shenhui, and may also have spent time as a student of Shenhui. But his attempt at reconciling meditation practice with the ideal of an immanent buddha nature that is only obscured by practice was shared with others of his generation. The Oxhead school, which also flourished in the late eighth century, produced texts that reconciled the apparent distinction between gradual and instantaneous methods of practice, including the *Platform Sutra* and the *Treatise on the Transcendence of Cognition* (the latter surviving in Tibetan translation in a Dunhuang manuscript).[12]

Thus it seems that there was nothing unusual in Moheyan's teachings for a Chan teacher from the late eighth century. His writings negotiated skillfully the balance of teaching meditation practices within a worldview in which there is no difference between the awareness of a buddha and that of an ordinary being. He was forgotten by the later tradition in China but, by several quirks of history, came to be the single representative of Chan, indeed of Chinese Buddhism in general, for the Tibetans.

ZEN IN TIBET

It is likely that Zen teachers played a role in the Tibetan assimilation of Buddhism during the period when Buddhism was adopted as the imperial religion, from the second half of the eighth century to the first half of the ninth. Unfortunately, we have no records from the time to confirm this. The only Tibetan historical accounts of the activities of

Zen teachers in imperial Tibet come from a single narrative compiled much later, probably in the eleventh to twelfth centuries. This narrative is known as the *Testimony of Ba,* named for the clan whose role in bringing Buddhism to Tibet is celebrated in it. The role of the *Testimony* is to create an origin narrative of Buddhist Tibet and, at the same time, give the Ba clan a major role in that narrative. This, and the fact that the text as we have it is several centuries later than the events it describes, makes it clear that the *Testimony* is not a reliable source for the events it describes. An early Dunhuang fragment of one of the stories in the *Testimony* shows how much it was altered over the centuries.[13]

Although they cannot be taken as reliable historical sources, the stories told in the *Testimony* about Chinese teachers are interesting when read in conjunction with the manuscripts. In the earliest complete version of the *Testimony,* all of these stories occur in the reign of Tri Song Detsen, one of the most successful rulers in the Tibetan imperial line, who expanded the borders of the Tibetan empire. The *Testimony* says almost nothing about his political activities, dealing only with his role as the founder of Buddhism as the state religion of Tibet. At the beginning of Tri Song Detsen's reign, Buddhism was at a low ebb in Tibet, unpopular with many of the powerful clan leaders, and it was partly in defiance of them that Tri Song Detsen, in his rise to power, came out in support of Buddhism. In the *Testimony,* the challenge facing Buddhism at the beginning of Tri Song Detsen's reign is represented by the expulsion of a Chinese monk from the temple at Ramoche. However, the monk leaves one sandal behind as a sign that he will return.

Some years later, when Tri Song Detsen is attempting to found a major Buddhist temple in Tibet, he invites an Indian scholar monk called Śāntarakṣita. However, due to problems caused by the local deities, the attempt to establish the temple is unsuccessful and the monk is sent back. Instead, three Tibetans are sent to China to find a Chinese teacher. According to the story, they meet a monk called Kim Heshang, who gives them instruction, and also have an audience with the Chinese emperor, who gives them a prophecy about the Buddhist activities of the Tibetan emperor. Whether these meetings ever took place, it is interesting that the Korean master Kim Heshang appears here, for he was otherwise forgotten in Tibet, and the references to him in the *Testimony* are highly obscure even in the time of the earliest versions that we have. However, he does appear in the Dunhuang manuscripts, as we will see later.

The last Chinese teacher to appear in the *Testimony* is the most important. Known to Tibetans as Heshang Moheyan (the first part of the name is simply the Chinese word for "monk" but used by Tibetans to mean "Chinese monk"), Moheyan was a popular teacher at the Tibetan court, but new problems arose for the Tibetan emperor as tensions developed between the different groups of foreign Buddhist teachers and their Tibetan disciples. According to the *Testimony,* the Indian teachers taught a graduated path in which the tantric and sutric teachings were carefully laid out as steps to enlightenment, whereas the Chinese emphasized the result rather than the path and a straightforward concept-free meditation rather than the multitude of methods offered by the Indian teachers.

When the tension between the Indian and Chinese camps threatened to erupt into violence, with some of the Zen disciples wounding themselves in protest and threatening suicide, Tri Song Detsen called for the situation to be resolved in a formal debate. The debate would decide which nationality, and which teaching method, would henceforth be supported by the monarchy and which would be banned from Tibet. The Indian side chose Kamalaśīla, a leading light in scholastic Indian Buddhism and the graduated path. The Chinese side chose Moheyan. The debate episode in the *Testimony* is clearly constructed from other sources; it begins with a brief exposition by Moheyan, a one-sided version of early Zen representing only the discussion of the immediate presence of enlightenment in the mind and omitting the discussion of how this is manifested in practice. This brief statement sets the scene for several pages of lengthy arguments for the validity of graduated practices, drawn from the written works of Kamalaśīla. Moheyan is not heard of until these arguments are finished, at which point he concedes defeat.

In the *Testimony,* the defeat of Moheyan results in Tri Song Detsen's giving his full support to the graduated practices and the Indian scholar monks who teach them. The episode is immediately followed by the establishment of a translation bureau to bring the entirety of the Buddhist scriptures into the Tibetan language. This proximity suggests that the main function of the account of the debate is to confer full authenticity on the Indian teachers and their Tibetan disciples who translated most of the Tibetan canon. Later, subsequent versions of the *Testimony* and other religious histories used the debate to make the point more clearly that India alone was the valid source of Buddhist scripture and that China was suspect, associated as it was with the "instantaneous" approach of Moheyan.[14]

As we have already noted, it would be naive to see this episode in the *Testimony* as having any documentary value. Though it came to be widely accepted in Tibet, it is not found in other early Tibetan histories, and when it does start to appear in other works, it is clear that the *Testimony* is the only original source. Furthermore, the story came to have a useful function in Tibetan religious life. As well as validating new lineages brought to Tibet from India as coming from the only genuine source of Buddhism, it served to confirm the importance of religious practice against those who emphasized the immanence of the enlightened state and immediate access to it. Thus the ultimate success of this debate story in Tibet owes much to its usefulness in subsequent centuries.[15]

This does not mean that no dispute ever took place. In 1952, the French Sinologist Paul Demiéville published a book based on a single Dunhuang manuscript: Pelliot chinois 4646, a collection of Chinese Zen texts including one called *Ratification of the True Principle of Instantaneous Awakening in the Greater Vehicle.* The manuscript consists of a series of questions and answers on Zen doctrines, with a preface by a student of Moheyan's called Wangxi explaining the background to these questions and answers. Wangxi relates how Moheyan was invited to the Tibetan court, where he granted a "secret Zen initiation" to the nobility. Moheyan's success at court seems to have been greatest among its women: one of the queens is said to have taken monastic vows, while the emperor's maternal aunt and thirty other women converted to Buddhism. After his departure from Tibet, the Indian teachers at the Tibetan court complained to Tri Song Detsen that the Chinese method was not a proper Buddhist path. In contrast to the Tibetan debate narrative in the *Testimony,* this did not lead to a single staged debate in Tibet, but rather a series of exchanges, by letter it seems, of questions posed by the Indian teachers and answers returned by Moheyan. The other major difference from the later Tibetan version is that Wangxi's preface concludes with an edict from the Tibetan emperor supporting Moheyan's teachings as genuine Buddhist practices.[16]

Wangxi's compilation of the questions and answers, and his writing of the preface, must have been done in the first half of the ninth century, and therefore predates the earliest version of the *Testimony* by at least two centuries. Thus Wangxi's version has at least a chronological authority over the Tibetan version. Yet it too cannot be accepted uncritically as documentary evidence. The questions and answers that are supposed to represent the letters sent back and forth between the Indian teachers and Moheyan look very much like many other question and answer texts found among the Zen manuscripts, which have nothing to do with hostile debates and everything to do with the way Zen was presented to a sympathetic audience. The questions in Wangxi's text generally set the stage for Moheyan's answers, just as in the Tibetan version of the debate, Moheyan's brief argument sets the stage for a lengthy refutation. Nevertheless, this account by Moheyan's students of this Zen teacher's having to defend his teachings at the behest of the Tibetan emperor (though not in a formal debate) may well be close to the truth, and is certainly closer than the later Tibetan version.

The records of monastic libraries from the early ninth century suggest that Zen was a known, but relatively minor, aspect of Buddhism at the Tibetan court, as they record only a handful of Zen manuscripts, including a "Zen Book" attributed to Bodhidharma.[17] It seems that Zen was still of significance to Tibetan Buddhists at the beginning of the tenth century, when the author Nub Sangye Yeshe—one of the few whose work survived the turbulent period following the collapse of the Tibetan imperial dynasty—wrote his *Lamp for the Eyes of Contemplation*. In this work, the "instantaneous approach" of Zen was accepted as a genuine Buddhist path but ranked only second in a hierarchy of four ways of approaching enlightenment: the gradual approach, the instantaneous approach, the tantric meditation of mahāyoga, and the formless approach of atiyoga. In particular, Sangye Yeshe was concerned that Tibetans were mixing up Zen and atiyoga, and as we will see later, there is evidence from the Dunhuang manuscripts that this was so.

In any case, several sources, including the Dunhuang manuscripts, but also the writings of Central Tibetan Buddhists like Sangye Yeshe, strongly suggest that Zen was not abandoned by Tibetans at the end of the ninth century as the later debate story claims. As we will see in the following section, there is evidence from Dunhuang that Tibetan Zen lineages were still flourishing into the tenth century. They were still active in the eleventh, when the Amdo master Aro Yeshe Jungne is said to have held two lineages, one Chinese and one Indian. And the contents of Zen texts were still known in the twelfth century, when Nyangral Nyima Özer discussed several key Zen works in his history of Buddhism in Tibet.

We have little or no specific historical data that would allow us to say anything for certain about the demise of Zen practices in Tibet. Yet I would suggest that it was more than anything else the pressures of the "later diffusion" of Buddhism in Tibet—the introduction of new practice lineages from India from the eleventh century onward, represented by influential teachers and authors like Sakya Paṇḍita—that led to the decline and eventual demise of Tibetan Zen. The new (*gsar ma*) schools based on Indic lineages were often quite aggressive in promoting India as the only source of the authentic dharma. In this environment, it would have been increasingly difficult for those holding Chinese lineages to assert their authority. Still, it seems that Zen texts and practices were being transmitted as late as the thirteenth century, when the Sakya master Künpang Chödrag Palzangpo was teaching them. And as late as the seventeenth century, the historian Tāranātha read a copy of the Tibetan Zen treatise *Drawn from Eighty Sutras*. Yet these seem to have been rare cases, long past the time when Zen played a significant part in Tibetan religion.[18]

ZEN AT DUNHUANG

There is no disputing the fact that Dunhuang is a long way from the centers of power in China, the capital cities of Chang'an (in the Tang period) and Kaifeng (in the Song), and Luoyang, with its many Buddhist monasteries. Henrik Sørensen has argued that the differences between the kind of Zen found in Dunhuang and the Zen that later sources tell us existed during the ninth and tenth centuries in central China is due to the distance between Dunhuang and these centers, and its political isolation after it was conquered by the Tibetan army in the late eighth century.[19]

Yet this isolation is perhaps overstated. After the Tibetan hold over Dunhuang was broken in the middle of the ninth century, Chinese monks did journey between Dunhuang and central China. We have the example of Wuzhen (816–95), who traveled to Chang'an to have an audience with the emperor, before returning to Dunhuang. I would suggest that we should consider the Dunhuang manuscripts to have been part of a local tradition of Zen, one that might have had its own peculiarities, but that we also consider that *all* Zen traditions were local. If other manuscript caches from the same period had been found at various locations in China, the local nature of the Dunhuang manuscripts would be more obvious, and the differences between their contents and the Zen described by the later tradition would seem less of an aberration. Also, scholars would perhaps be more careful about using the Dunhuang manuscripts as straightforward sources for "Tang Dynasty Zen," which would not be a bad thing.[20]

Since few of the Zen manuscripts from Dunhuang are explicitly dated, it is difficult to be certain of when they were written. Daishun Ueyama has suggested three periods for the manuscripts: (i) Chinese manuscripts from roughly 750–80, either brought from central China or written on imported paper, (ii) Chinese and Tibetan manuscripts from the period of Tibetan occupation, roughly 780 to 850, written on locally made paper, and (iii) Chinese manuscripts from the late ninth and tenth centuries, written on local paper. This periodization is really only relevant to the Chinese manuscripts. The Tibetan conquest cut off the Tang dynasty's trade route through Central Asia and probably did stem the flow of manuscripts from the center. Even after the fall of the Tibetan empire and the reconquest of Dunhuang and the surrounding area by local Chinese rulers, the situation did not revert to what it had been before the Tibetan conquest, as the Tang dynasty was severely weakened, and finally fell in the early tenth century.[21]

However, Ueyama's schema is based on a misconception about the Tibetan Zen manuscripts. Like most previous studies of Tibetan Zen, he assumed that the manuscript sources date from the period of the Tibetan occupation of Dunhuang; yet much of the Tibetan material from Dunhuang has now been dated to after the end of the occupation. In fact, as we have seen, Tibetan Zen survived into the tenth century and beyond. In the light of the fact that the Tibetan Zen manuscripts from Dunhuang come from exactly the same period as most of the the Chinese ones, that is, the ninth and tenth centuries, and were also produced locally, we should be looking at Tibetan and Chinese Zen not as two different traditions but simply as Zen practices presented in two different languages.

So who was practicing Zen at Dunhuang? There were no Zen monasteries at this time, so here as elsewhere in China, Zen was taught and practiced in Buddhist monasteries among other Buddhist practices.[22] When we take this into account, it is not surprising to find that many manuscripts containing Zen texts also have texts from other traditions, and some texts appear to combine Zen with other traditions. Rather than regarding this as a phenomenon of "hybrid" or "syncretic" Zen, it would be better to consider that Zen was not at this point distinct enough as a tradition for its textual separation from other genres to be the norm.

From the cave in Dunhuang, there are roughly three hundred manuscripts containing Chinese Zen texts, and a little over fifty containing Tibetan Zen texts, and the range of texts they contain is similar:[23]

1. Apocryphal sūtras and commentaries upon them. These are sūtras thought to have been written in Zen communities, some of which were translated into Tibetan from Chinese.
2. Treatises on Zen doctrines in the form of questions and answers, the answers explicating and defending Zen positions, usually with quotations from sūtras. Some treatises appear more like dialogues, resembling more the "encounter texts" of the later Zen tradition.
3. Treatises discussing Zen practices of teaching and meditation, or explicating the instantaneous versus gradual issue. These are sometimes but not always by named authors.
4. Brief sayings of Zen masters, often collected into anthologies of several masters.
5. Accounts of masters in a lineage, often containing elements of 2, 3, and 4 above.
6. Poems on the enlightened state.[24]

The arguments made above about not abstracting texts from their contexts should help us to understand that a classification like this is helpful but will be misleading if we do not immediately return to the manuscripts from which these texts have been abstracted. When we do, the first thing to notice is that the texts were rarely copied into manuscripts alone; they were usually copied, and used, as parts of a compendium of texts. And thus we should also note that texts that would not normally be considered "Zen texts" per se, such as the *Vajracchedikā sūtra* (in Pelliot tibétain 116), a general explanation of Buddhist meditation (in IOL Tib J 709), or a treatise on Buddhist philosophical views (in IOL Tib J 121), are unequivocally Zen texts when found in these compendia. A fascinating composite Chinese manuscript Or.8210/S.4037 contains Zen material along with a prayer for the dedication of merit to recite after having chanted a sūtra, a eulogy to the *Lotus Sutra,* spells for various occasions, and on the other side, a circular for a local lay Buddhist society. Aggregations of texts like this show us that distinctions of genre have very little to do with how people actually lived and practiced.[25]

So a quite different list, which might help us to approach the texts better in terms of their function, would be a list of uses of manuscripts. The following is an incomplete attempt at a list of uses of Buddhist manuscripts from Dunhuang:

▸ Group initiation rituals, as discussed earlier in connection with Pelliot tibétain 116
▸ Teaching, in small groups or in the context of larger gatherings, such as initiation rituals
▸ Rituals performed for various worldly needs (for example, medical, funerary, divinatory)
▸ Daily recitation or meditation practice of scriptures and other texts, individually or in groups
▸ Students' notes and writing practice
▸ Communication aids, such as glossaries and phrasebooks
▸ "Receipts" of ritual activity, such as sponsoring or copying scriptures
▸ Amulets and talismans
▸ Antiquarian collecting

The vast majority of the Chinese Zen manuscripts are written in cursive, somewhat rough handwritings, and often contain errors, which suggests that they were not the work of professional scribes working for patrons, as were many of the Buddhist scriptural texts. Rather it seems that most Zen manuscripts were created by students and teachers for many of the functions described in the list just above. We can probably get a bit further than this by looking closely at the writing styles of the Tibetan manuscripts. Elsewhere I attempted a classification of the most common writing styles found in Tibetan manuscripts from the Tibetan imperial period (that is, up to the mid-ninth century) and compared these to the styles seen in the later manuscripts (mid-ninth to tenth centuries). Certain handwriting styles, along with other archaic features, allow us to place otherwise undated manuscripts in this early period; other styles are found only in the later period, and some of these are characteristic of the last phase of the Dunhuang manuscripts, the late tenth and early eleventh centuries.[26]

There is more variance in the quality of writing in the Tibetan Zen manuscripts. Carefully and evenly written manuscripts like Pelliot tibétain 116 and IOL Tib J 710 clearly come from a different context than roughly written manuscripts like Pelliot tibétain 121. While the former may have been created as prestige items (which is not incompatible with their being used in ritual practices), the latter are probably personal copies of texts, copied out by students, either from dictation or from other written models.[27] It is also sometimes possible to identify individual handwritings, and this can show us the variety of texts that could written by the same scribes who wrote the Zen manuscripts. This reminds us that the category of "Zen text" is an artificial, and somewhat arbitrary, way of drawing a line around the manuscript collection and that the people involved in creating and using these manuscripts created and used many other sorts of Buddhist manuscripts.

It is worth considering whether these functions that we are considering might be linked to the particular physical form of the manuscript in question. The connection between use and physical form, though not much discussed in textual studies, is central to archaeology, where in the absence of texts, human practices must be deduced from objects alone. This attention to the materiality of the manuscripts can help us to understand textual artifacts as well, for in this case too, "the mechanical properties of artefacts either enable or constrain their use in certain social practices."[28] In less technical terms, one could say that there is a "fit" between the way things are designed and the uses to which people put them.

A useful way of thinking about this is the concept of *affordance*. The affordances of an object are what it allows people to achieve with it: an elongated object of moderate length affords wielding, a rigid object with a sharp edge affords cutting and scraping, a graspable rigid object affords throwing, an elongated elastic object affords binding, and so on. As objects are designed for more and more specific purposes, their affordances become more specific as well. Thus *affordance* includes both the person and the object, both society and its artifacts. For our purpose of trying to understand the uses of texts as practices, we can look at the physical features of manuscripts in terms of which kinds of activities they afford.[29]

Most of the Tibetan manuscripts from Dunhuang are either scrolls, pothi (loose palm-leaf-style folios), concertina (the folded form also known as *leporello*), or stitched booklets (the codex). Let's consider which book form works best for a sermon or initiation ritual. There is some advantage in choosing the concertina form for a manuscript like Pelliot tibétain 116, which contains several texts in a specific order to be used in a ritual. While loose-leaf pothi pages can get mixed up, a concertina keeps the pages, and the texts, in the right order. Even if you are extracting or summarizing from your materials, it is important to know exactly where in the ritual you are.

How about personal recitation practice? If one is sitting in front of a support for the text, a scroll, pothi, or concertina would all work fine. The scroll would require the most manual work in rolling and unrolling, while the pothi and concertina need only be turned every two pages. The pothi probably offers the most affordance for this purpose because loose-leaf pages simply sit flat. And for note taking and other ad-hoc writing practices, booklets and small concertina manuscripts are easy to carry, facilitate looking up texts, and can be held in the hand when standing or sitting without a place to put the book down. However booklets are less good in a situation where one is sitting or standing in front of a support for the manuscript, as they are less likely to sit flat, and the pages need to be turned more often. Other uses might be associated with different forms; amulets, for example, often take the form of small sheets of paper with a religious text or spell written on them.

This kind of detail might seem superfluous to some, but these small-scale activities—the practices of reading, teaching, taking notes, per-forming ceremonies, and so on—are the forms of life in which the texts are brought into being. Texts function only in their physical instantia-tion as individual manuscripts, and it is in the collective of people and artifacts, and the practices that bind them, that we will best understand them.

1

ORIENTATIONS

THE FORMLESS PRECEPTS

As we saw in the introduction, the largest manuscript collection of Tibetan Zen texts is Pelliot tibétain 116. This concertina manuscript begins with two canonical Buddhist texts, the *Prayer of Excellent Conduct* and the *Vajracchedikā sūtra*. These texts are followed by a very brief overview of the differences between the greater and lesser vehicles, a popular theme among the Tibetan Zen texts, and a short explanation that the correct "view" (a technical term for a doctrinal position) is the sameness of all entities. After this we have three substantial Zen texts, the centerpiece of the manuscript. The first of these is called *Treatise on the Single Method of Nonapprehension,* a substantial compilation of quotations from sūtras, the first part of which is translated here. This is followed by further collections gathering together the teachings of eighteen masters of meditation, and a translation of a popular Chinese Zen text that is also found in the Chinese manuscripts from Dunhuang. Finally, short texts round off the collection: a discussion of problems that might arise in meditation practice and their remedies, and a song on the ultimate state of reality.[1]

The nature and order of the texts in Pelliot tibétain 116, along with the fact that it was well used and repaired, suggest that its function was related to the ceremony of conferring the precepts of the bodhisattva incorporating an initiation into Zen meditation practice, and it is in this context that we should read the *Treatise on the Single Method of Nonapprehension* (referred to hereafter as the *Single Method*). This ritual is also represented in the *Platform Sutra,* where the folding together of bodhisattva precepts with the Zen ethos of nonconceptualization (drawing heavily on the *Vajracchedikā*) is known as the "formless precepts."

The sixth and fifteenth questions of the *Single Method* provide another clue that the function of this text and manuscript is the conferring of the formless precepts. The sixth addresses the concerns of those who worry that "it is improper to instantaneously cultivate nonconceptual concentration straight after generating the awakening mind." The fifteenth addresses the claim that "if you first generate the awakening mind by means of conceptual analysis, you can accomplish nonconceptualization later." The generation of the awakening mind (*bodhi*) is the essential practice of the bodhisattva precepts; as the two questions imply, in the Zen ritual, it is immediately followed by an initiation into the kind of nonconceptual meditation that is described in many other Zen texts.[2]

MISCELLANIES AND MOVABLE TEXTS

The *Single Method* is composed of three parts: (i) fifteen questions and answers addressed to those who are attached to substantial things (*dngos po*) and terminology (*sgra*), with citations from scripture, (ii) twenty-one questions and answers about Buddhist concepts in the context of nonconceptualization (*rnam par myi rtog pa*), with citations from scripture, and (iii) a précis of the teachings of several meditation teachers.[3]

As well as the other copies of the *Single Method,* there are other very similar collections of questions and answers that overlap significantly with it. A text preserved in the Tibetan canon and attributed to the famous Indian translator Vimalamitra, *The Meaning of Nonconceptual Meditation,* contains some very similar questions, with correspondingly similar scriptural citations, often in the same order, but with different commentary in between the citations. The similarities are enough that one text seems to be a reworking of parts of the other. Yet there are a sufficient number of other similar yet different question and answer texts found in the manuscripts (for example, Pelliot tibétain 821) to make it seem that new texts were created by reworking existing collections of questions and answers, so that none of the extant texts can be identified as the original.[4]

These Zen miscellanies contain elements that are transferable and found in other configurations elsewhere; depending on their nature, we call some of these transferable elements "texts" and others "parts of texts." The term "intertextuality" seems tailor-made for a case like this; we cannot speak of "authors" here so much as a stock of questions answered by scriptural citations that have been arranged in different ways in different texts.[5] The citations also seem to have circulated alone, and they may have been the basic units of teaching practice. The texts are miscellanies, made up of nested parts that may be found elsewhere in other combinations. So, for example, the *Single Method* is a text found in several miscellanies, but it itself comprises three sections, and each of these sections comprises distinct parts (questions and answers or quotes from masters). The whole text, individual sections, and individual parts are also seen in other settings. Thus the boundaries of the text are difficult for us to fix, which suggests that "the text" is not necessarily the best concept to be applying here. Perhaps the discrete boundaries of a text were not the most important consideration when the manuscripts were written; rather what was important was the task of gathering together material suitable to a purpose.

An important thing to recognize here is that teachers and their students rarely used scriptural texts in their entirety (and the longer the text, the more likely this is to be the case). Instead a much more limited corpus of excerpts from sūtras was used. Like popular miscellanies in other cultures, these manuscripts have been neglected in favor of the study of complete (canonical) texts, yet they are more revealing of the way texts are made use of in everyday life.[6] As I suggested in the introduction, the way the texts are arranged in Pelliot tibétain 116 probably follows (or one could equally say, determines) the order of the initiation ritual, but that does not mean that each text was read out in its entirety. Rather they would probably have been used as source material to be drawn upon in the course of the ritual. The occasional marginal marks, usually crosses (+) in the texts at the beginning, also suggest that a teacher was extracting parts of the texts to use in sermons.

QUESTIONS AND ANSWERS

If the function of the *Single Method* in the larger context of Pelliot tibétain 116 was as source material for a sermon as part of a Zen initiation ceremony, then the way that it is arranged as answers to questions seems well suited to its purpose. The question and answer format has a long history, with precedents in Indian Buddhist literature as well as Chinese pre-Buddhist texts. At the most general level, the format of posing questions and giving answers is a useful way of organizing one's material. In the case of the *Single Method,* the fact that many of the questions express doubt or critique and are answered with quotations from scriptures suggests something more. The text is defining, and at the same time, defending, a method of practice; it suggests that what is being presented is something out of the ordinary, or at least new and subject to uncertainty among its audience. It is, thus, well suited to an initiation into a new way of practice. The text, drawn upon in a sermon, works to orient the audience to the ethos of this system.[7]

The fifteen questions in the first part of the *Single Method* all begin with the words "some say" followed by a position that is challenged by the answer and the scriptural citations. The reliance on scriptural authority is very different from the later formulation of the essence of Zen as a "separate transmission outside the scriptures." Given that the context here is not a debate but an introduction to the approach of Zen, it seems that the audience must have been expected (i) to be new enough to the Zen approach to need this kind of orientation, yet (ii) to know enough about Buddhism to understand the terminology and to accept the authority of the quoted scriptures.

The audience, then, would have been monks or Buddhist lay people. The sentence that introduces the text states its dual purpose of refuting those who have a problem with the Zen approach and instructing those who accept it: "This has been written in reply to the objections of those who have, from the beginning, been attached to substantiality and terminology, and for the sake of those yogins who repudiate that view and whose practice is free from subject and object." Since it is unlikely that those directly hostile would form the majority of attendees at an initiation or sermon, we can take these two types as being indicative of the liminal status of the audience, not hostile, but not yet insiders either.

So, what is the "nonapprehension" of the text's title? "Apprehension" (Tib. *dmyigs*, Skt. *upalambha*) here refers to perception, specifically to the perception of "features" (Tib. *mtshan ma*, Skt. *lakṣaṇa*). Features are the characteristics of phenomena imputed by the deluded mind, including their existence as substantial entities (Tib. *dngos po*, Skt. *vastu*) separate from the mind. Thus the first line of the text states that it is directed against those "attached to substantiality and terminology." The latter term (Tib. *sgra*, Skt. *śabda*) indicates that what is at stake is also the intellectual aspect of Buddhist learning, such as the enumerations of the Abhidharma and Yogacāra literature (both of which are well represented among the Tibetan texts from Dunhuang). Thus nonapprehension is a transcendence of the ordinary way of conceptualizing experience but also of intellectual methods within Buddhism itself. The approach is very much based on that of the Perfection of Wisdom sūtras, such as the *Vajracchedikā sūtra* with which Pelliot tibétain 116 begins.

Most of the questions pose challenges to this ethos of nonconceptualization, from a more conventional reading of Buddhist practice. This is put in the most general terms in the first question. In general, greater vehicle Buddhist texts distinguish between the "accumulations" of merit and wisdom, the first being accumulated through meritorious practices such as making offerings, the second through nonconceptual meditation. These are often considered to be complementary, but the *Single Method* argues that the accumulation of wisdom is in itself sufficient for the accomplishment of enlightenment. Or rather, more subtly, it suggests that the accumulation of merit is encompassed by the accumulation of wisdom. This is essentially the same point made in the third question (and in several other Tibetan Zen texts) about the six perfections: the sixth, wisdom, is said to encompass all of the other five. However, the *Single Method* does allow for practice as well. The answer to the fourth question states that "those who read and those who have given up reading are both performing the precious accumulation of merit."

MANUSCRIPT AND TEXT

The *Single Method* is the most well-represented Tibetan Zen text among the Dunhuang manuscripts, with five other versions extant in other manuscripts, and it appears to have been composed in the Tibetan language (although many of its individual elements may have been translated from Chinese). It was also, apparently, known in Central Tibet: a very similar title is found in the late imperial library catalog *Pangtangma*. Despite the many manuscript copies of the *Single Method,* no complete copy survives, though previous studies have incorrectly taken the version in Pelliot tibétain 116 to be complete, missing the note on the last panel by the person who repaired the manuscript. Referring to the *Single Method* by another name, *The Little Lamp,* the note states that the last two panels were present but damaged and, presumably, removed:

> In *The Little Lamp,* two panels are not present. Anyone who makes a copy of the book should include the two missing panels. This is not an omission: the two complete panels were not present.

On the back of the same panel, we can see the same scribe's note about where the missing text should be, marked by a cross between two lines: "The two missing panels should be included here." The notes show that the person who carried out the repair knew that part of the text was now gone and expected others to know enough to insert it where it was missing in the manuscript.[8] In the translation here, I have taken the beginning of the missing third question from a parallel passage in *The Meaning of Nonconceptual Meditation* and then filled the remainder of the gap from the first two panels of another copy of the *Single Method* found on the verso of Pelliot tibétain 823. This leaves some doubt as to whether there was more material in the answers to the second and third questions, but we do now have all of the questions, and at least most of the answers of the complete text.

A Text on the Single Method of Nonapprehension:
Written Merely to Support Great Yogins in Remembering the Answers to Doubts

This has been written in reply to the objections of those who have, from the beginning, been attached to substantiality and terminology and for the sake of those yogins who repudiate that view and whose practice is free from subject and object.

QUESTION: Some say that those who cultivate only the accumulation of wisdom cannot attain full and perfect buddhahood, and this is because they do not practice the accumulation of merit, which is conditional. This is the explanation:

We do not render all of the teachings of the tathāgata meaningless. From the *Prajñāpāramitā sūtra*:

When generosity and the rest are practiced without the three spheres (of agent, action, and object), they are transcendental perfections.

Thus it is not prohibited for those who cultivate only the accumulation of wisdom to accomplish unsurpassed enlightenment. "What is the evidence for this?" From the noble *Candrapradīpa sūtra:*

> If you experience one dharma, then the entire accumulation of enlightened qualities will be complete, and you will swiftly achieve unsurpassed enlightenment. What is this "one dharma"? When you know that all dharmas are thusness in their very essence, then all dharmas are without designation, and all terminology is abandoned.

From the *Sañcayagāthā sūtra:*

> For those who train in the perfection of insight, all of the perfections will be encompassed by that.

From the *Suvarṇaprabhāsa sūtra:*

> From the basis of the precious dharmakāya concentration, the dharma of buddhahood will arise. Noble child, this nonconceptual dharmakāya is not eternal, nor does it cease; it is the middle way.

As these sūtras say, if one cultivates the single accumulation of wisdom, unsurpassable enlightenment will manifest spontaneously. If this practice gets mixed up with the perception of features, then it will have the defect of not transcending saṃsāra. From the *Laṅkāvatāra sūtra:*

> Compounded features are not possessed by the buddhas. They are the qualities of a wheel-turning king, but he is not called a buddha.

Thus it is evident that if one cultivates the single accumulation of wisdom that is unmixed with features, this is the supreme path.

QUESTION: Some say that it is improper not to be learned. This is the explanation:

From the *Laṅkāvatāra sūtra*:

"Being learned" means studying the meaning, not the words.

As it says, this is not to be accomplished through thinking . . .⁹

QUESTION: Some say that it is necessary to practice the six perfections. This is the explanation:

From the *Vajrasamadhi sūtra*:

A mind that does not move from emptiness embodies the six perfections.

Also, from the *Brahma-viśeṣacinti-paripṛcchā sūtra:*¹⁰

Not thinking is generosity. Not abiding is morality. Not making any distinctions is patience. Not accepting or rejecting is effort. Nonattachment is concentration. Nonduality is insight.

As this shows, the six perfections are embodied within an unmoving mind. If the mind chases after generosity and the rest, then it will have the defect of not transcending saṃsāra. From the *Laṅkāvatāra sūtra*:

For as long as there is mental engagement, there will be worldly materialism.

As it says, if one conceptualizes features, one will not transcend saṃsāra.

QUESTION: Some say that not chanting, reading, writing, and keeping one's vows is improper. This is the explanation:

From the *Mahā-uṣṇīṣa sūtra*:

Cultivating insight for a single day and night is of immeasurably greater merit than writing, reading and chanting sūtras for millions of eons. Why is that? Because it goes beyond birth and death.

As it says, there are many gates to the truth, including being a yogin or being someone who reads and listens to the sūtras, so those who read and those who have given up reading are both performing the precious accumulation of merit.

From the *Vajracchedikā sūtra:*

The dharma of which I speak is like a boat. If one should abandon even the dharma, what more need be said about that which is not dharma?[11]

Those who do a lot of reading and writing have the defect of being stuck in the yoga of a beginner. If they believe in the gate to the truth and cultivate it, then their practice will become much better.

QUESTION: Some say that it is improper not to apprehend all the roots of virtue in order to dedicate them toward enlightenment. This is the explanation:

From the *Sañcayagāthā sūtra:*

Since it is true that "even the true nature of things is not to be dedicated," if one thoroughly understands this, that is a proper dedication. If one creates features, there is no dedication. Where there are no features, there is dedication toward enlightenment.

This shows that engagement without features is itself a dedication toward enlightenment. If one makes a dedication by methods involving apprehension, this is a defect.

From the *Sañcayagāthā sūtra:*

The Conqueror has said that apprehending the white dharma is like eating good food mixed with poison.

This shows that making dedications by methods involving apprehension is of no great benefit.

QUESTION: Some say that it is improper to instantaneously cultivate nonconceptual concentration straight after generating the awakening mind. This is the explanation:

From the *Prajñāpāramitā sūtra:*

Straight after generating the awakening mind, one should apply the mind to total comprehension.

From the *Mahā-uṣṇīṣa sūtra:*

At the point when the meaning is instantaneously understood, everything is instantaneously purified. Substantialists do not have instantaneous cessation; instead they have gradual purification.

From the *Jñānālokālaṃkāra sūtra:*

I have taught the interdependence of causes and conditions, and I have explained gradual engagement. However, I said this as skillful means for deluded people. How could there be gradual purification in this spontaneously accomplished dharma? When the nature transcends limits, what is there to see by distinguishing parts? When you do not assert the tiniest thing, then your mind is the sky, and the buddha is one with the objects of your experience.

From the *Jñānācintya sūtra:*

Just as much as sentient beings train, that is how much they see. Just as much as sentient beings train, that is how much they hear.

From the *Laṅkāvatāra sūtra* again:

It is like this, Mahāmati. All forms, which are like reflections in a mirror, appear instantaneously and nonconceptually. Just the same, Mahāmati, is the Tathāgata. The stream of mental appearance for all sentient beings is nonconceptual, and objects of experience that lack appearance are instantaneously purified.

This shows that it is proper to cultivate nonconceptualization from the beginning. If you think "I'll attain the meaning of nonconceptualization at some later point," you will become lazy.

From the *Sañcayagāthā sūtra:*

This person might say, "I will not attain supreme enlightenment until Mount Meru has crumbled." However, if he gets discouraged just thinking about the scale of this, then the bodhisattva becomes lazy.

So, saying that it is improper to cultivate nonconceptualization from the beginning is like not allowing the donkey to be beaten by the stick that is used for the ox: it is clearly not the correct practice.

QUESTION: Some say that it is impossible to bring benefit to sentient beings while abiding in concentration on emptiness. This is the explanation:

From the *Prajñāpāramitā sūtra:*

As for this, Subhūti, when a bodhisattva mahāsattva is abiding in the three concentrations, any sentient beings experiencing dualistic discrimination are established in emptiness. Any sentient beings experiencing features are established in the nonexistence of features. Any sentient beings experiencing intention come to experience the nonexistence of intention. Subhūti, a bodhisattva mahāsattva who experiences the perfection of insight and abides in the three concentrations brings sentient beings to spiritual maturity.

As this shows, the methods of the profound dharma bring about extensive benefits to sentient beings, but teaching the dharma by means of features only spreads misfortune. This same sūtra also states that to teach the dharma as a method that apprehends everything is to be a friend of misfortune. This shows that teaching the dharma to sentient beings by means of features is to teach an erroneous path.

QUESTION: Some say that it is improper not to recollect the three jewels. This is the explanation:

From the *Prajñāpāramitā sūtra:*

> To realize the nonsubstantial nature of all phenomena is to cultivate the recollection of the Buddha. If one has no recollection and no mental engagement, this is recollecting the Buddha. This is recollecting the dharma. This is recollecting the sangha.

This shows that not engaging mentally is to recollect the Buddha who is reality itself. Recollecting the Buddha by means of apprehension is to obscure nirvāṇa. From the *Prajñāpāramitā sūtra:*

> Even a brief mental engagement with the Buddha is a feature, and if even this is an obscuration, then how much more so any other kind?

This shows that generating recollection of the Buddha by means of apprehension is of no great benefit.

QUESTION: Some say that external objects that are nonmental exist separately. This is the explanation:

From the *Ghanavyūha:*

> From the forms that exist on earth to the palaces that abide in the god realms, whichever of the variety of things manifests, it is the manifestation of basic consciousness (*ālaya*).

From the *Laṅkāvatāra sūtra*:

> Bodies, possessions, and abodes are all the manifestation of basic consciousness to humans.

This shows that all internal and external phenomena arise from the mind. If it is claimed that they exist separately from the mind, this is the fault of having an inferior view. The *Laṅkāvatāra sūtra* says that the principle of mind is disputed by those with wrong views. And from the same sūtra:

> When one attaches a term to something, that term is imputed to reality itself. Those who superimpose upon things will, after death, fall into the lower realms.

This shows that claiming that objects exist separately from the mind is not a valid view.

QUESTION: Some say that in ultimate truth wisdom has only a momentary existence. This is the explanation:

From the *Laṅkāvatāra sūtra*:

> The mental consciousness that grasps forms and shapes arises along with the five compounded consciousnesses; since they do not abide even for a moment, I have explained them to be "momentary." When the all-ground consciousness that is known as "buddha nature" (*tathāgatagarbha*) arises momentarily alongside the mind, it is momentary due to the imprints of consciousness, but due to the uncontaminated imprints, it is not momentary.[12]

Also, from the *Vajracchedikā sūtra*:

> Subhūti, since there is no apprehending the mind of the past, future, or present, there is no mind.

This shows that wisdom is not ultimately momentary. If you claim that wisdom is ultimately momentary, you will destroy the dharmakāya.

From the *Laṅkāvatāra sūtra:*

> Gold, diamonds, and relics of the Conqueror are indestructible due to their special purity. If the higher knowledge was momentary, then the noble ones would lose their nobility. Yet the noble ones do not lose their nobility.

The claim that wisdom is ultimately momentary is no more than a claim that exists in foolish intellects. When this claim is tested in the definitive scriptures, it shows that wisdom is not accepted to be momentary.

QUESTION: Some say that enlightenment can be attained only after three countless eons. This is the explanation:

From the *Saṃdhinirmocana sūtra:*

> The imprints of bad states of being are purified in three uncountable eons, or in a year and a month, or in half a month, or in a day and night, or in a day, or in a meditation session, or half a session, or in a moment, a second, a limitless eon.

This shows that there is no single time that it takes to attain enlightenment.

QUESTION: Some say that it is improper not to make composite offerings and the like. This is the explanation:

From the *Ratnakūta sūtra:*

> When there is no discrimination of the Buddha, no discrimination of the dharma, and no discrimination of the sangha, that is the purest offering.

Thus it is not improper for a yogin not to make composite offerings and the like.

QUESTION: Some say that it is improper not to confess one's sins and purify wrongdoing. This is the explanation:

From the *Mahāmokṣa-diśunpuṣya-krokramtya sūtra:*

Someone who wants to purify wrongdoing should sit up straight and look perfectly. By doing so, perfection itself is perfectly viewed. If one sees perfection, one will be liberated. This is the supreme purification of wrongdoing.

This shows that cultivating the unmoving is the best kind of purifying confession.

QUESTION: Some say that it is improper for a person who meditates on the path not to rely on antidotes. This is the explanation:

From the *Gaganagañja sūtra:*

When phenomena are completely pacified, there is no need for antidotes.

This shows that if you do not conceptualize mental features, there is no need to rely on antidotes.

QUESTION: Some say, about generating the awakening mind, that if you first generate the awakening mind by means of conceptual analysis, you can accomplish nonconceptualization later. This is the explanation:

From the *Mahā-uṣṇīṣa sūtra:*

If one first generates a mind that is created and ceases, then the final result that is beyond creation and cessation will not be attained.

From the *Prajñāpāramitā sūtra:*

> Once beginners have generated the awakening mind, they should commence training in the nonapprehension of all phenomena.

Also, from the *Buddhakośa sūtra:*

> Since phenomena are free from discrimination, only wisdom that is without features is capable of perceiving their origin. Thought and analysis are not capable of cognizing it.

This shows that practicing the method of conceptual analysis is a mental activity directed only toward features and that there is never any benefit in conceptualizing space, which is without creation or cessation.

CONCLUSION

The above has been set down briefly as a reply to those who have faith in features. This can also be grasped from the texts on yoga. The preceding answers are merely teachings aimed at those who instigate superficial debates, but those who have reached the limit of perfection do not cling to their own texts or refute those of others, just as they do not accept nirvāṇa or reject saṃsāra.

MASTERS OF MEDITATION

SPEECH ACTS

From a very early period, Zen texts have been based on the teachings of previous masters. While the nature of the actual historical teachings that these masters might have given and even the fact of their historical existence has been questioned in modern scholarship, from the point of view of practice, what is important is how these teachings were used. Within a tradition, the significance of a figure and the words attributed to him or her are unaffected by later judgments as to whether he or she actually existed and ever said such things. As John McRae provocatively puts it: "It's not true, and therefore it's more important."[1]

The collection of masters' teachings translated here is found in the manuscript Pelliot tibétain 116, directly after the *Single Method* (translated in chapter 1). As we have seen, Pelliot tibétain 116 seems to have been put together as an aid to the performance of a Zen initiation. The *Single Method* provides an orientation to the Zen ethos for students who are familiar with Buddhist concepts and accept the authority of Buddhist scriptures. What then is the role of these masters' teachings? At first glance, what we see in the teachings of Master Moheyan and eighteen other teachers is the same kind of statement repeated over and over in slightly different ways. It reads as repetitive, with a great deal of redundancy. But then this manuscript was not meant to be read. It was meant to be used in a ritual, and if we want to appreciate how this text would have worked, we have to try to understand its role in the ritual.

If these teachings were part of a public ritual, probably a sermon in the context of an initiation, then we must regard them as performative utterances, as "speech acts." That is, the speaking of these words will be the performance of an action, with a socially understood effect upon those taking part in the ritual. In the terminology suggested by J. L. Austin in *How to Do Things with Words*, they are *performative* in that they are intended to bring about a change in the world. In this case, they are part of the words of a ceremony that will produce people who are permitted and committed to undertake Zen Buddhist practices, just as the utterance of the words of a wedding ceremony produces people who are permitted to partake in, and committed to, the social institution of marriage.[2]

It is not surprising, then, that here, as in many rituals, there is repetition and redundancy. We may describe the language of rituals using a distinction discussed by John Searle: it is not an attempt to *fit the words to the world*, but rather to *fit the world to the words*.[3] A simple assertion or description can be performed once, but an attempt to affect a change in the world may need to be repeated many times. The effect of the ritual is to transform the participant, and the words are agents of transformation. So, these teachings should not be read merely as descriptions, although they may look like they are when presented to us as mere texts. The words here attributed to Zen masters are not generally as explicitly transformative as "I now pronounce you man and wife," but they may still have functioned to change their listeners. Bruno Latour, making a similar point about Christianity, compares religious talk to love talk:

> "Do you love me?" is not assessed by the originality of the sentence—none are more banal, trivial, boring, rehashed—but rather by the transformation it manifests in the listener, as well as in the speaker. *In*formation talk is one thing, *trans*formation talk is another. When the latter is uttered, something happens. A slight displacement in the normal pace of things. A tiny shift in the passage of time. You have to decide, to get involved: maybe to commit yourselves irreversibly.[4]

So we should be aware that our current reading habits—reading statements like these as descriptions or sources of information—may be very different from how the texts were used in the past, as a part of the performance of a ritual. As a performance, we should consider how each master's teachings might effect a transformation and how they worked cumulatively in proximity to each other.

POETICS

What then is the transformation that these teachings are intended to effect in the listener in the course of a ritual? We have no direct commentary upon them that would make this explicit, but in the repetition of the same themes again and again, a certain structure emerges. These short texts-within-texts are all quite similar to each other; they are working within conventions, which are apparent in their limited vocabularies, repeating themes, and similar structures. The texts must to some extent follow these conventions if the audience is to respond to them in the right way.[5]

Of course we cannot put ourselves in the place of those who took part in the ritual in which these texts played a part, but by placing ourselves at least in an attitude of sympathetic receptivity, we can discern patterns in the repeated themes of the Zen masters' teachings. Perhaps the most obvious pattern is the repetition of negation, in which a series of terms, including thought (*bsam*), conceptualization (*rtogs*), recollection (*dran*), and apprehension (*dmyigs*) are invoked only to be negated. The cumulative effect is to place these kinds of mental activity in an entirely negative light. The personal transformation involved is the production of practitioners who believe this to be true and accept an ethos in which practice is only genuine when free from conceptualization. This is communicated with vivid imagery in the teaching attributed to Pabshwan:

> One who touches instantaneously the truth of nonconceptualization is like the king of the lions, and with the roar of a lion, he will be fearless in all kinds of activity. Those who accomplish division and apprehension are like baby foxes. Making distinctions and conceptualizing differences, they are unable to achieve buddhahood. These fools are empty and weak.

Yet the texts as a whole do not rest with this absence of mental activity; instead it is immediately filled with genuine practice and realization, which is spontaneously present when not fettered by conceptualization. Such presentations of what is apparently a negation as a positive aspect of Buddhist practice and realization is present in many teachings here, including the text attributed to Moheyan, which shows how the ten perfections of greater vehicle Buddhist practice are present in the practice of sitting in nonconceptualization. Similarly, the brief teaching attributed to Wuzhu turns the three negations usually associated with this teacher into positive aspects of the conventional Buddhist path: "Not thinking is morality, not conceptualizing is concentration, and not giving rise to the illusory mind is insight."

Three levels of understanding are implicit here: first, a naive understanding of practice that is conceptual and oriented to an externalized result; second, the negation of this understanding of practice in the mere absence of thought and the presence of buddhahood; and third, a deeper understanding of practice based on this. Some version of these stages can also be seen in the Perfection of Wisdom literature, including the *Vajracchedikā sūtra* that begins Pelliot tibétain 116. In the Perfection of Wisdom literature, the absence of conceptual elaborations is known as emptiness (*sunyatā*), and while emptiness is not specifically invoked in the teachings of the Zen masters here (except in negative terms by Shenhui), it is implicit in them. John McRae has identified these same three levels in Chinese Zen texts from the Oxhead school, which he describes thus:

> An expression of Buddhism is made in the first element, the terms of the expression are erased in the second element, and the understanding of Buddhism is thereby raised to a new level of profundity in the third element.[6]

We might perhaps add a fourth aspect to the teachings here, a celebratory tone in the statements about the result of true practice, for example at the end of the teaching attributed to Shenhui:

> This is the totally perfect *dharmakāya*, equivalent to the space of reality, the same as the sky. Since it is by nature nonabiding, its qualities are limitless and spontaneously perfected.

Here, for a receptive audience, the emptiness of the negative rhetoric (with which Shenhui's teaching also begins) and the filling up of this emptiness with a new nonconceptual form of Buddhist practice culminate in a realization that everything sought in practice is already present. This is the instantaneous aspect of these teachings: that which is conceived of as being at the end of a long process of practice is here right now if practice is conceived correctly; or in the words of the master Kengshi: "If you understand the meaning, you will be a buddha in the time it takes to snap your fingers."

This fourth, celebratory, aspect of the teachings is also the culmination of the text series in Pelliot tibétain 116 as a whole, which ends with a poem entitled *A Brief Teaching on the Space of Reality*. Similarly, in the *Platform Sutra,* Huineng's initiation ceremony ends with his *Song of Formlessness,* which his lay audience is encouraged to recite and put into practice at home. The platform sermon of Shenhui also ends with songs celebrating the enlightened state. In this way, these rituals end on a positive note, so that the transformation in every participant culminates in the generation of the emotional energy to continue to practice after the ceremony has ended.[7]

Finally, while I would argue that all of these levels are present in the Zen masters' teachings found in Pelliot tibétain 116, we shouldn't expect a linear progression from one level to the next when we read them. They are all simultaneously present, and this structure only appears by accumulation. Thus the repetitiveness that results from gathering these short teachings together is not a fault; it is how their poetics is impressed upon their audience.

THE MASTERS

What we have here in Pelliot tibétain 116 is a brief text attributed to Moheyan followed by a series of quotations ascribed to eighteen meditation masters, each quotation described in Tibetan as "drawn from the sayings of so-and-so" (*mdo las 'byung ba*). The Tibetan word "Shenshi" follows many of the names; this is simply a transliteration of the Chinese honorific *xiansheng* following the contemporary Chinese pronunciation (closer to modern Japanese *sensei*). These masters follow directly after the *Single Method,* and since that text ends with the teachings of eight Buddhist masters, there is a natural continuation here in the arrangement of the texts for a ceremonial sermon. The eight masters at the end of the *Single Method* are (i) Nāgārjuna, (ii) Bodhidharma, (iii) Wuzhu, (iv) Xiangmo Zang, (v) Artanhwer, (vi) Wolun, (vii) Moheyan, and (viii) Āryadeva. This is an interesting list. It is not chronological and does not fit any known Zen lineage, but it does give a context.

The first and last teachers are Nāgārjuna, the foundational figure of the Madhyamaka approach, and his student Āryadeva. This brackets the other masters within the ethos of the Madhyamaka, which informs much of their writings. The other masters are Wuzhu, the teacher from Sichuan who founded the Baotang school; Xiangmo Zang, a student of the famous Shenxiu and a teacher of Moheyan; Artanhwer, an Indian meditation teacher known only from the lineage history written in Pelliot tibétain 996, but apparently well known in Tibetan (but not Chinese) Zen; Wolun, a master whose teachings seem to have been popular during the ninth and tenth centuries but was later largely forgotten; and Moheyan, who, here and elsewhere, is a central figure of Tibetan Zen.

The masters' teachings here include a few of the same teachers: Wuzhu is here, as well as the teacher whose lineage he claimed to represent, the Korean master Kim. Moheyan appears among the eighteen masters as well as in a separate text that precedes them. And a relatively long passage is attributed to Shenhui, who is best known for his polemics against teachers of the "Northern School" such as Shenxiu and Xiangmo Zang. The presence of Xiangmo Zang in the *Single Method* indicates that this polemical background was of little importance to the compilers of manuscripts like Pelliot tibétain 116. As suggested in chapter 1, their work is best seen as the gathering of materials suitable to a purpose. The distinctions between schools and factions appears to have been of much less interest to practitioners than it was to doxographers.

The majority of the masters quoted here are unknown to the later tradition, although their names seem to be transliterations of Chinese names. Further comparisons with the Chinese manuscripts may lead to more of them being identified in the future. Many of them are found in another Tibetan source, the *Lamp for the Eyes of Contemplation.* In this work, the masters are cited as examples of the "instantaneous approach," with much the same text as found here in the manuscript. Some of the order of the manuscript is retained in the *Lamp* as well. This shows at least that this arrangement of masters' teachings was well known enough to be drawn upon by a Central Tibetan writer in the late ninth or early tenth century. Other teachers are also quoted in the *Lamp* who have not survived in the Dunhuang manuscripts in Tibetan translation but are extant in the Chinese originals. This suggests that the collection of masters' teachings represented here may also have been taken directly from a Chinese source.[8]

A Brief Teaching on How the Six or Ten Perfections Are Included in Nonconceptual Meditation, by Master Moheyan

1. When sitting in nonconceptualization, since you have completely renounced the three spheres (of agent, action, and object), great generosity is completely present.
2. When sitting in nonconceptualization, since the faults of the three gates (of body, speech, and mind) do not arise, great morality is completely present.
3. When sitting in nonconceptualization, since you are patient in the nonarising of discrimination, great patience is completely present.
4. When you don't cut off the flow of nonconceptualization, which is like a river, great effort is completely present.
5. Since nonconceptualization is concentration, great concentration is completely present.
6. Nonconceptualization itself is insight: since this is the wisdom that transcends the world, great insight is completely present.
7. Since nonconceptualization is the method that takes you to the unsurpassable state, great method is completely present.
8. When sitting in nonconceptualization, since you conquer the three realms, great strength is completely present.
9. Nonconceptualization is aspirational prayer: since you aspire to engage in the aspirational prayers of the tathāgata, the great aspirational prayer is present.

10. Since nonconceptualization is the space of the tathāgata, great wisdom is completely present.

FROM THE MAXIMS OF MASTER BUCHU (WUZHU)

As for morality, concentration, and insight: not thinking is morality, not conceptualizing is concentration, and not giving rise to the illusory mind is insight. This is the mnemonic.

FROM THE MAXIMS OF
MASTER KIMHUN (KIM HESHANG)

When mind is in equanimity, all phenomena are equal. When you know perfection, there is no phenomenon that is not buddha. When you understand the meaning, mental states of attachment and desire do not arise. If you have experience of the perfect field of perception, there is nothing to look for. How is that? The suchness of the perfection of insight is primordial equality, and therefore it is not apprehended.

FROM THE MEDITATION MAXIMS OF
MASTER DZANG SHENSHI

The nonarising of conceptual recollection is the complete perfection of meditation. Having no attachment to the objects of the six consciousnesses is the complete perfection of insight. When meditation and insight are perfected in this way, nonconceptual insight is born. Through this, you go beyond the three spheres (of agent, action, and object).

FROM THE MEDITATION MAXIMS OF
MASTER DEULIM SHENSHI

One who meditates on the path ought to possess the eye of the mind. Without conceptualizing or apprehending anything, nothing is accomplished: mind is in equanimity, and this is the "eye of the mind." When you are in this state of nonconceptualization, apprehension based in attachment to the forms of objects perceived by the eyes is liberated. The ears, nose, tongue, and intellect are similarly liberated; this is known as "the six independent kings." This is the site of liberation. Liberation is buddha.

FROM THE MEDITATION MAXIMS OF MASTER LA SHENSHI

If meditating on the path, you find the essence of awakening, you will rest in perfect relaxation of the body, and your mind will be spacious and even like the sky. At this point, form and all of the other conditions of the six objects will not become harmful disturbances. This is the dharmakāya of the tathāgata.

FROM THE MEDITATION MAXIMS OF MASTER KIMHU (KIM HESHANG)

If a person meditating on the path is free from all concepts of a view, this is "the unique experience." When you have this experience, none of the afflictions that come from habitual imprints can arise. This is the path of liberation.

FROM THE MEDITATION MAXIMS OF MASTER PABSHWAN SHENSHI

One who touches instantaneously the truth of nonconceptualization is like the king of the lions, and with the roar of a lion, he will be fearless in all kinds of activity. Those who accomplish division and apprehension are like baby foxes. Making distinctions and conceptualizing differences, they are unable to achieve buddhahood. These fools are empty and weak.

FROM THE MEDITATION MAXIMS OF MASTER PIR SHENSHI

In a mind that is in single equanimity, no phenomena arise. This is the path of liberation.

FROM THE MEDITATION MAXIMS OF
MASTER DZWAI SHENSHI

When the parched earth of the habitual afflictive emotions is watered with the spring water of perfection, the seeds of enlightenment will grow. Seeing the nature of this, you will swiftly attain buddhahood.

FROM THE MEDITATION MAXIMS OF
MASTER TSHWAN

A monk meditating on the path should examine the experience of peace. In this experience, there is no possibility of being tied in the knots of the afflictive emotions.

FROM THE MEDITATION MAXIMS OF
MASTER WANG SHENSHI

If you know one phenomenon, then you will be unmistaken about all phenomena. If you don't know one phenomenon, then you will be mistaken about all phenomena. This is known as "the experience of perfection." It is knowing the dwelling place of the mind. In this experience, none of the habitual mental afflictions arises. It is like this: when you pour cold water into boiling water, the boiling is stilled.

FROM THE MEDITATION MAXIMS OF
MASTER DZWANGZA SHENSHI

When one who is meditating on the path looks at the buddhahood of the Buddha, by seeing the Buddha, they approach the Buddha, step by step. If they do not look at the Buddha, then not seeing the Buddha, they move away from him, step by step.

FROM THE MEDITATION MAXIMS
SENT BY MESSENGER FROM THE CHINESE LAY
PRACTITIONER KENGSHI

When you are meditating on the path, strive with heartfelt diligence. If you understand the meaning, you will be a buddha in the time it takes to snap your fingers. If you don't understand it, then you will not attain buddhahood for as many eons as there are drops of water in a river. If you know the instantaneous meaning of the greater vehicle, this is known as "proclaiming the great sound of the dharma." All sounds that are apprehended and conceptualized are cleared away. This is liberation.

If you don't know the meaning, that is known as "the sound of dark confusion." All of the faults of habitual afflictive emotions instantaneously arise. These are the chains of saṃsāra. When a lion is born, from the first moment, he walks in the manner of a lion, and giving a lion's roar, overcomes the sound of all other animals. This is like knowing the instantaneous meaning. When a fox is born, from the first moment he walks in the manner of a fox, and makes the sound of a fox, but is despised by all the beasts of prey, and because they know his weakness, he is fearful. All of this unhappiness coming together instantaneously is due to not knowing the instantaneous truth.

FROM MEDITATION MAXIMS OF
THE MEDITATION TEACHER SHINHO (SHENHUI)

Accomplish the sign of truth, which is to be always without recollection. What does this mean? The nature of thought is primordially a nonresting essence. It is not to be obtained, nor can it be apprehended by thought or meditative absorption. It cannot be apprehended as "this is thought" or "this is not thought" or good or bad or as thought's having color and shape. Nor can it be apprehended as having limits or not having limits, as having size or not having size, as having a place or not having a place. Do not apprehend any of the features of mental activity.

If by doing this, you do not rest upon thought, then that primordial nonabiding in the essence of thought's sameness is intrinsic awareness. Awareness means coming to rest in nonresting. For example, a bird flying through the open sky goes without resting. If it did rest in the open sky, it would fall. In the same way, it is not possible for there to be no awareness. Without awareness you would fall into the extreme of emptiness. Therefore nonresting is the primordially peaceful essence. Through the wisdom of the patriarchs, you are able to be aware of the essence of this rare peace. If you apprehend this directly, there is no mental activity in that apprehension. If you see it directly, there is no mental activity in that seeing. This is the totally perfect dharmakāya, equivalent to the space of reality, the same as the sky. Since it is by nature nonabiding, its qualities are limitless and spontaneously perfected.

FROM THE MEDITATION MAXIMS OF BYILIG HWASHANG

Birth-and-death and nirvāṇa are primordially nondual. Neither together nor separate, neither happy nor unhappy. What is this? It is known as "the transcendence of saṃsāra and nirvāṇa."

FROM THE MEDITATION MAXIMS OF MASTER MAHAYAN (MOHEYAN)

Birth-and-death and nirvāṇa are primordially nondual. Neither together nor separate, neither happy nor unhappy. What is this? The sameness of saṃsāra and nirvāṇa is known as "transcending saṃsāra."

FROM THE MEDITATION MAXIMS OF MASTER DEU SHENSHI

Cleansing the mind does not require water. Practicing generosity does not require wealth. With a perfect mind, you will accomplish the dharma. By sitting up straight, you will see the Buddha.

FROM THE MEDITATION MAXIMS OF MASTER BUCHU (WUZHU)

The perfect mind makes the maṇḍala. The fire of no features burns the incense of liberation. Then we practice unobstructed repentance. Then we practice morality beyond thought, contemplation without any achievements, wisdom without duality. We do not ornament the maṇḍala with worldly causality.

He also taught: All sentient beings are pure from the beginning. Since they are perfect at the beginning, there is nothing to add, nothing to subtract. When you follow after thoughts, the three worlds are contaminated by the mind, and you are born into a sequence of aggregated bodies. If you follow a virtuous friend, and see the nature, then you will achieve buddhahood. If you are attached to features, you will cycle. It is because sentient beings have thoughts that we teach without thoughts that designate. When there is no thought, one does not even rest in nonthought. The mind of the three realms does not reside on the level of personal peacefulness. It does not reside in features. It is not even nonactivity. Where there is freedom from illusion, there is liberation.

The existence of mind is like waves on the water. The nonexistence of mind is a heresy. Following after birth is the stain of sentient beings. To rely on peacefulness is to move toward nirvāṇa. Not following after birth, not relying on peacefulness, not entering contemplation, you will not be born. Not entering meditation, you will not be born. Hold the mind! Do not scatter! There are no substances or shadows, so do not rest in features or the lack of features.

TEACHERS AND STUDENTS

INSTANTANEOUS AND GRADUAL

The tension between instantaneous and gradual approaches to enlightenment is very evident in the Zen manuscripts, both Tibetan and Chinese, and in the memories of Zen in later Tibetan history. The tension is implicit in most early Zen texts and is arguably addressed in the very first, Bodhidharma's *Two Entrances and Four Practices.* However, it became a topic of explicit discussion during the eighth century, in the sermons of Shenhui, who aligned himself thoroughly with the side of the instantaneous approach, against the gradualist practices he called "the Northern School."

This tension was also discussed by Zongmi, who recognized that it actually involves two questions, one about practice and the other about realization. The first question is whether a single practice, such as "observing the mind" or just sitting in formless meditation, is sufficient for the achievement of enlightenment, or whether a variety of practices is required. The second question is whether enlightenment comes suddenly, in an all-or-nothing scenario, or whether it is a process of gradual awakening. Now, it would seem that these two should be aligned, in that a single method should be associated with sudden enlightenment, and a multitude of methods with a gradual process of awakening. But, as Zongmi notices, this is not necessarily the case. It is also possible to have a single method that entails a gradual awakening and equally to have a multitude of methods leading to a sudden awakening. As we will see, the text translated here seems to favor the second position.[1]

The instantaneous/gradual dichotomy was also central in the later Tibetan understanding of Zen, informed by the Tibetan version of the debate between Moheyan and the Indian teachers. In this story, Moheyan is presented as firmly on the side of the instantaneous approach, to an extent not seen in the writings of any Zen master from the period, even Shenhui. Thus the authors of the Tibetan debate story align Chinese Buddhism with the instantaneous approach and Indian Buddhism with the gradual approach, a simplification that enables the narrative to avoid the fact that both aspects are present in Indian Buddhism, especially in the Perfection of Wisdom scriptures that were held in great esteem by those on either side of the debate.

In fact, the antigradualist rhetoric of Shenhui was an exception in early Zen, and even his own students began to soften his polemical stance, which may have worked well in sermons, but lacked guidance for Zen monks and lay practitioners. Other new movements, such as the Oxhead school, that developed in the wake of Shenhui's polemics also explored the ground between instantaneous and gradual approaches. Many of the Tibetan Zen texts also share this feature. The works of Moheyan are much subtler than the caricature in the Tibetan debate story. Thus the negotiations of the tensions in practice and realization are present in both Chinese and Tibetan Zen, and the latter derives them principally from its Chinese sources.[2]

TEACHERS AND STUDENTS

The text translated here is a guidebook for meditation instructors. In the Tibetan text, these are referred to as teachers, or more literally, "friends" (*bshes gnyen*, Skt. *mitra*); this term is present from early Buddhist texts, and its full form is "virtuous friend" (*dge ba'i bshes gnyen*, Skt. *kalyāna-mitra*). Though it is occasionally used to refer to relationships with peers, most often it refers to the personal relationship between a teacher and student, in both monastic and lay Buddhist contexts. In the manuscript Pelliot tibétain 116, the texts arranged for the Zen initiation ceremony are also instructive; a significant part of these ceremonies was the sermon. However, giving a sermon to a crowd is not the same thing as giving personal instruction to an individual, and the materials gathered for these two purposes might be quite different.

The guidebook for teachers translated here is the first text in the manuscript IOL Tib J 710. This is a complete manuscript containing two texts; the second, *The Masters and Disciples of the Laṅka School,* is translated below in chapter 4. This manuscript was carefully and skillfully produced, on high-quality paper, in a clear and neat version of the Tibetan headed script, with the pages numbered sequentially. It was probably written by a professional scribe or a monk with scribal training. The handwriting appears to be one of the later Buddhist styles seen in the Dunhuang manuscripts from the tenth century. Thus it may well have been written later than Pelliot tibétain 116, but we can tell that it eventually came into the possession of the same person who repaired Pelliot tibétain 116, as the same handwriting covers the back of the final folio. Whereas in Pelliot tibétain 116 this person replaced missing parts of the manuscript, and some of the text, here the manuscript is complete and he has added some supplementary material, extracts from sūtras stating that all phenomena are the Buddha, that to practice correctly is to see the Buddha, and that this seeing is buddhahood itself. These extracts complement the two main texts in the manuscript.

The first text in the manuscript, the one translated here, has no title, and begins and ends rather abruptly, although the manuscript appears to be complete. Thus it looks like an extract from a longer text. From the contents of the text, it seems that the extract was selected because it deals with specific issues arising for Zen teachers in assigning meditation practices to students and guiding their practice. The main issues dealt with in this extract are negotiating the tension between instantaneous and gradual approaches to meditation, and dealing with the visions that arise in the course of students' meditation practice.[3]

HOW TO TEACH MEDITATION

In the text translated here, the problem of reconciling instantaneous and gradual approaches to practice and realization is not a doctrinal question. It is a problem that arises and is addressed in the context of teaching meditation. Scholastic writers like Zongmi are concerned with setting out the positions of various schools, perhaps in an overly formalized way, and this can lead to the view that these issues are about doctrine. In the text here, on the other hand, we see the same issue in the context of practice, specifically from the point of view of the teacher. As a guidebook for teachers, this text addresses practical problems that teachers face in training their students to be proficient in meditation. It is therefore quite different from the polemical rejections of practice by Shenhui, or Zongmi's thoughtful but highly scholastic account of the doctrines of Zen schools.

The dilemma for Zen teachers is that the essence of one's mind is inherently enlightened, and yet beginners in meditation have a variety of different personality types that prevent them from realizing this. Therefore, in practice, the ideal of a single instantaneous method is not always appropriate:

> Meditating on the same thing may not be suitable for each and every mind. In their confusion, some people are happy, some wild, and some drowsy, while others are a mixture. . . . The instantaneous approach is not the full story; it is needed for some, but not for others.

The example used to illustrate this is drawn from medicine. A doctor prescribes different cures for different ailments, and a skilled doctor will know just what a patient needs. Likewise, a skilled teacher guides a student in using the appropriate "antidote"—a meditative method used to combat a specific harmful tendency. Like a doctor's prescription, the teacher's method must be followed rigorously; a student who takes different advice from many teachers, or who simply makes things up, will go astray. Proper practice also takes time. One passage, which gives the impression of drawing on long experience of teaching, cautions that those students who seem to take to meditation straight away sometimes drop out later on, while others who do not seem to be well suited to meditation keep on going until they become skilled meditators.

In the end, though, the result is the same. In the medical metaphor, the doctor may use different methods for different illnesses, but the joy of being cured is always the same. When realization comes, it is the same for everyone, and it comes all at once:

> The blessings of the buddhas are not gradual like the growth of plants or the performance of a piece of music. Like the reflection of a face in a mirror or the sun dawning immediately over the land, the imprints are purified instantaneously.

Thus the teacher is to teach various methods, with a skillful sensitivity to what individual students require, but as long as they work hard at meditation, they will all reach the same point, and when realization comes, it will be a swift dawning. Most important, perhaps, is the passage that emphasizes the need for teachers to remain with their students for the length of their meditation practice, whether it be days, weeks, or even years. The text states that "if [students] receive correction early on, they will certainly get to the point of meditation. If this doesn't happen even in the mind of a single person, then what is there to say about the multitude of sentient beings?" Here the lofty ambitions of the sūtras, and many other Zen texts, are brought down to earth in the relationship between the teacher and a single struggling student.

The other issue faced by teachers that this text deals with is the vivid experiences that students report in the course of their meditation, some of which, like visions of buddhas, seem to be good signs. The text takes a pragmatic view of this. If such visionary experiences cause the meditator to become arrogant and overconfident, this is obviously a problem. So they should be taught that these visions are like dreams. On the other hand, since visions are actually a sign of progress in meditation, if a student does not experience any signs of progress like this, it is actually a problem. Thus the teacher's assessment of these reports of visions must depend on the personality of the students, the practices they are engaged in, and their progress in meditation. Here again we get the impression that the text is genuinely concerned with the exigencies of teaching rather than setting out a particular doctrinal position.

THE GREAT YOGA

The actual practice of meditation that is invoked in this text is known either as "tathāgata meditation" or "the great yoga." Both terms show that this text, as with many other Tibetan Zen texts, draws heavily on the *Laṅkāvatāra sūtra*. Tathāgata meditation is invoked as the fourth and highest method of meditation in the second chapter of the *Laṅkāvatāra sūtra*:

> Also, Mahāmati, there are four kinds of meditation. What are the four? The meditation practiced by the childish, meditation that distinguishes the meaning, meditation that apprehends thusness, and tathāgata meditation. . . . Mahāmati, what is tathāgata meditation? One who stands on the ground of the tathāgata, through abiding in the joy of the three signs of noble discerning wisdom, accomplishes the benefit of countless sentient beings. Thus I call this "tathāgata meditation."[4]

The sūtra itself is not clear on whether all four kinds of meditation are considered valid stages in a graduated practice, or whether the first, second, and third are merely inadequate forms of meditation to be avoided. The polemical Zen teacher Shenhui is said to have taught tathāgata meditation as the only correct meditation practice, according to his biography in the *Record of the Dharma Jewel through the Generations*:

> The Venerable Shenhui of Heze Monastery in the Eastern Capital [Louyang] would set up an [ordination] platform every month and expound on the Dharma for the people, knocking down "Purity Chan" and upholding "Tathāgata Chan."[5]

It is equally clear that Zen texts like the one translated here invoke tathāgata meditation, neglecting the other three types, as the immediate and unmediated practice of the highest form of meditation. The aim of this text seems to be to retain this ethos while allowing for other, more pragmatic meditation practices to be given to students as well.

The *Laṅkāvatāra sūtra* is also the source of the term "the great yoga," though the failure to recognize this has caused some confusion in the study of Tibetan Zen. The great yoga (Tib. *rnal 'byor chen po,* Skt. *mahāyoga*) is better known as the name of a genre of tantric practice known in the Nyingma school of Tibet, and in the Dunhuang manuscripts. This other use of the term "the great yoga" has led some scholars to see its use in the Tibetan Zen texts as an allusion to tantric practice, or even to suggest that these Zen texts were masquerading as tantric texts.[6] In fact, in the *Laṅkāvatāra,* the phrase "a yogin of the great yoga" (*mahāyogayogin*) is used repeatedly in reference to a person of the highest insight into the nature of reality. For example:

> Lord of Laṅkā! These princes, the yogins of the great yoga, are skilled in subduing false teachers, clearing away wrong views, and refuting the view of a permanent self. They are skilled in transforming intellect and awareness. This is the commitment of those who practice the greater vehicle.[7]

In the text here, tathāgata meditation and the great yoga are synonymous with each other. As the last part of the text makes clear, they refer to a meditation in which there is no dualism between awareness or wisdom and its object. While this is the best form of meditation, the text also makes clear that it is not the first kind of meditation a student should practice. It is to be practiced after more conceptual and directed types of meditation, referred to here as the meditations of the hearers or bodhisattvas, the kind of practices involving the antidotes that are to be prescribed to a student depending on his or her particular mental state. These two, hearers and solitary buddhas (Skt. *śrāvaka* and *pratyekabuddha*), are archetypes of the Buddhist practitioners who have not accepted the teachings of the greater vehicle, and the practices and realizations of Zen are often set out in opposition to the more limited (if not entirely misguided) approach of these "lower" types.

TRANSLATION

Like thieves who cannot get near to a man of great wealth, or the gathering of clouds that is dispersed by a great wind, erroneous concepts should be reduced and diminished over and over again. Those who enter the great yoga are intrinsically aware that the essence of mind is by nature uncreated and unceasing. Since those two concepts are delusory, when they are understood to be mere designations, what need is there to do anything with the concepts that remain? Mind is purified instantaneously, not gradually.

Hearers with sharp faculties rely on methods with features, such as visualizing skeletons and decomposing corpses. Bodhisattvas rely on methods without features, such as the three gates to liberation. They subdue all features with a single antidote, yet they are unable to abandon the antidote itself. Those who enter the great yoga of the tathāgatas are empowered with wisdom, so their perceptions are nonabiding, like an optical illusion. Analyzed phenomena are uncreated, and because they are uncreated, they are also unceasing.

The wisdom of the hearers and solitary buddhas is like a mirror inside its cover. The wisdom of the bodhisattvas is like a mirror wrapped in a net. The wisdom of the buddhas is like a mirror without a cover: they are have no distractions, and because they are not obscured even by concentration, their personal qualities are unceasing and spontaneously bring about the benefit of sentient beings.

How do we deal with the faults that make true meditation impossible? Meditating on the same thing may not be suitable for each and every mind. In their confusion, some people are happy, some wild, some drowsy, while others are a mixture. If they are to improve, one method will not be suitable for all of them. Since there is an uncountable number of antidotes, there is one suited to whatever arises in the mind of a sentient being. The instantaneous approach is not the full story; it is needed for some, but not for others. Where there are many teachings, there are many concepts and much confusion, so it is inappropriate to show all the different ones to every yogin. It is better to explain just the parts that are needed.

This is like the way a patient is cured by a doctor. When a skilled doctor examines a particular patient and applies medicine and rituals, his objective is attained and the patient is helped. A highly skillful doctor can even cure the patient from a distance. But if an unskilled doctor applies the medicine and the rituals however he wants, then the patient will not be helped, and the sickness may get worse. Similarly, if an incapable teacher teaches whatever he likes, or if a student follows a variety of highly skilled teachers but makes up his own path, it will not be enough. This is an erroneous path, and a waste.[8]

For that reason, teachers should stay with their yogins as they meditate, asking them about their practice and state of mind, and getting to know them thoroughly. Then if they receive correction early on, they will certainly get to the point of meditation. If this doesn't happen even in the mind of a single person, then what is there to say about the multitude of sentient beings?[9]

For days, months, and years, mornings and afternoons, right from the beginning, yogins must strive. If they occasionally fall down or stand up, then their teacher should look after them. The minds of these yogins should be honored and protected like one's own eyes. Some of them understand meditation right from the beginning and seem to be capable but later fall back and fail to grasp it. Some find it difficult to understand at the beginning and seem incapable, yet they strive right to the end and become skilled in true meditation without the slightest tendency to cling to meditative experiences.

The aspects of conceptualization that are most powerful should be corrected individually with their antidotes. In the end, however, there is only one true meditation, and the happiness that is purified of concepts is of one taste. It is like the way different illnesses are purged by specific medicines, yet the happiness of recovery is the same experience for all illnesses. However, while a single concept may be completely purified using a certain method, it is still necessary to purify other kinds of concepts gradually. Therefore one should not try to accomplish the eight meditations all at once; one should engage in them successively.[10] Trying to purify all the various concepts at once is like trying to count every grain of sand on this great earth.

Furthermore, an instantaneous cessation by a single antidote for those who don't understand the essence of mind will be of no benefit. The hearers' and solitary buddhas' absorption in cessation quickly and roughly covers the mind with dharma, but due to an inconceivable number of subtle imprints, they do not get beyond birth and death. The hearers claim that there are existents, comprising eighty-one subtle particles, and that by apprehending any one of them, it is possible to cut off all features. Yet because mind is dualistic, when it apprehends one thing, it does not apprehend anything else. Thus when it apprehends emptiness, that emptiness can obscure names and other features. But since it is without features, emptiness cannot obscure that which is without features. Therefore, features are the obscuration of seeing things as existent, and emptiness is the obscuration of seeing things as nonexistent. In either case, enlightenment and the supreme wisdom of the hearers are incompatible.

In graduated practice, you first make external objects empty and then eliminate the features of the internal mind gradually, starting with the largest. Though you will eventually attain freedom from features, you must not give up this practice until you attain the bliss of intrinsic awareness. However, purifying a multitude of false concepts over a long period is itself a mental concept. If you carry on in this way until the end of the eon, you will still be afflicted by negative forces which trip you up. So it will take a very long time.

In instantaneous practice, all external appearances are understood to be merely mind, and the internal mind is nothing more than imagination with mistaken concepts. When you have become proficient in nonsubstantiality, you can maintain these two as emptiness. This is not, however, the nonexistence of each and every thing. The buddha of reality itself transcends arising and cessation without ever changing. The intrinsic awareness of this instantaneously purifies all appearances from inside out, without falling back. This takes only a short time.

When they are immature, foolish people grasp at the features of their mistaken apprehension. They think that all mental phenomena and those that derive from the mind are faulty up until the achievement of great nirvāna. This is not the point of the great yoga. Tathāgata meditation overpowers all concepts without conceptualizing nonconceptualization, based on a method in which features neither exist nor do not. It engages in the wisdom of the noble intrinsic awareness, free from the imprints of negative states of existence. The blessings of the buddhas are not gradual like the growth of plants or the performance of a piece of music. Like the reflection of a face in a mirror or the sun dawning immediately over the land, the imprints are purified instantaneously. This is also taught in all the scriptures.

When bodhisattvas attain forbearance toward this uncreated dharma, in between the view of self and the supreme wisdom, they reside in and practice the perfection of insight without attaining or not attaining it. Let us deal with those who object to this: "If enlightened conduct is to liberate all unenlightened sentient beings before myself, and yet I remain a solitary sage, renouncing the welfare of the rest of you, how does that work? That would be to fall into the paths of wrongdoers, the two lower vehicles and the heretics." Don't worry about this. Mere generosity is understood even by hell-beings, and even hearers and heretics practice virtues like morality and contemplation. Even so, they are still like blind people. None of their paths is capable of bringing them to the wisdom of the body of reality itself (*dharmatākāya*) and the wisdom of nonself. Because they can't reach it, they cycle in the three realms of existence. If I cycle round in that way without being liberated, then clearly I will not be able to bring about the great welfare that benefits others.

How should we examine the various signs that arise in meditation? When a vision appears before the eyes of a great yogin, it can be the bodies of buddhas and bodhisattvas, or it can be in the form of spirits and demons. Since all appearances are like a fairy city, it is unreasonable either to view them as good qualities or to become fearful. When something like this appears, pride arises in thoughts like "Because of my great powers, I see emanation bodies and magical signs appear; based on this, I should be ranked alongside the noble ones!" Or "This is a sign of accomplishment!" Anyone who desires such things violates the supreme wisdom of the buddhas. The great yogin will be overpowered by demons.[11]

Furthermore, if certain yogins do want to see buddhas manifest, the blessings of the buddhas will fulfill this wish, and reflections of the buddhas' bodies will certainly appear. However, since the buddhas' bodies are without birth and cessation, all of my visions are nothing more than the perceptions of my own mind. Thus they are like dreams, and I should not desire them. On the other hand, if reflections of the buddha bodies do not arise for a yogin and no signs appear, that is not necessarily good either. Why? Because no such visions appear to all those various beings who are disturbed by mistaken concepts, yet they are not in accord with the contemplation on the tathāgata. This is due to their great karmic obscurations.

By analogy, the reflection of the sun or the moon can appear in an ocean or a stream but not among rocks or in the midst of waves. Among those practicing inner discipline, there is a difference between those of high, middling, and low abilities. If visions arise for those who are diligent and disciplined, it should be considered a problem. If they arise for middling types, they should be seen as signs of success. If no signs appear for a distracted person, it should again be considered a problem. Thus one cannot say whether signs in general are good or bad. It is important for a skilled teacher to distinguish between the different mindstreams, practices, and meditative qualities.

If yogins focus on features not emerging and purify their minds through nonconceptualization, then they will see buddhas and bodhisattvas, and signs will arise for those who hope for them. Great yogins who have no hopes for attainment and do not abide anywhere provide no basis for illusions to appear. Equally, buddhas obviously do not make delusory displays for those who are unsuitable for training. When the reflections of other beings and the variety of features are viewed as the mind, it is reasonable that they should not be seen at all. If such things are occasionally seen, it is a corruption of tathāgata meditation. It will be because they have mixed in other contemplations or because of harmful visions caused by the demon Māra. Therefore what arises from the results of concentration should be incinerated by the fire of supreme wisdom that does not desire any such signs, whether they be the forms of buddhas and bodhisattvas or mountains, lakes, lotuses, and lights.

Is tathāgata meditation without error? Those who engage in the great yoga do not examine mind using supreme wisdom. They do not examine the aggregates using the dharmakāya. Nor do they look for entities other than the mind and the aggregates to examine. They do not even examine wisdom itself using supreme wisdom, nor do they examine the dharmakāya itself using the dharmakāya. They know that what is beyond all extremes is not the same as the phenomena of the three realms.

Ordinary beings conceptualize things as arising and abide in arising. Hearers and solitary buddhas do not abide in arising, but they do abide in cessation. Bodhisattvas abide happily in the wisdom of noble intrinsic awareness, without the arising and cessation of any phenomena. The supreme wisdom of the tathāgata does not even abide in the forbearance of the dharma that engages in nonarising and noncessation and the happiness of intrinsic awareness. Therefore this approach should come after the concentration of the bodhisattva. It is also suitable to come right after the hearers have refuted the non-Buddhists and attained the heat and peak levels of the path of preparation.

This will not arise or be found among the objects perceived by gods and humans. It is not a cause to be achieved or a result to be attained. Therefore those who strive in the great yoga do not search within all phenomena and nonphenomena; they are above that. Then what is the method by which the tathāgatas comprehend nonself? It can be known by one with great power of mind.

The Practice of Genealogy

THE TRANSMISSION OF THE LAMP

The *Masters of the Laṅka* is one of several early Zen lineage accounts that later fell into obscurity but were nonetheless part of a trend toward what would later become Zen orthodoxy. That is, they situated Zen practice in the context of a lineage brought to China by the Indian monk Bodhidharma and thereafter handed down from one master to another, like the way a flame is passed on by lighting one lamp from another. That metaphor, which makes an early appearance in the *Masters of the Laṅka,* was chosen for the title of the Zen lineage account called *Record of the Transmission of the Lamp*, which was written in 1004 and became one of the central texts of Zen. Due to the lasting fame of this text, the genre of Zen lineage writing has come to be known as "transmission of the lamp" literature.[1]

The origins of Zen lineage writing are in the Chinese Buddhist genre of biographies of eminent monks. These collections of biographies, the first of which was written in the sixth century, have more in common with Chinese secular histories than with Indian Buddhist writing.[2] In the seventh century, Chinese Buddhist schools such as Tiantai began to define themselves through the construction of transmission lineages. Then in the early eighth century, the first two Zen lineage accounts, the *Masters of the Laṅka* and the *Record of the Transmission of the Dharma Jewel,* were written, and later in the same century, the *Record of the Dharma Jewel through the Generations.*[3] One thing that makes the *Masters of the Laṅka* different from these other Zen lineage accounts written around the same time is the fact that the whole lineage is predicated on a single scriptural text, the *Laṅkāvatāra sūtra*. This was not unusual in Chinese Buddhism—the Huayen school is named for the *Avataṃsaka sūtra* and the Tiantai school was also known as the school of the *Saddharmapuṇḍarīka*.

However, this was not the way things developed with Zen, which came to be characterized by the famous phrase "a special transmission outside of the scriptures." Though that definition was not widely accepted until after the tenth century, both the *Record of the Transmission of the Dharma Jewel* and *Record of the Dharma Jewel through the Generations* are closer to it in spirit than the *Masters of the Laṅka* in basing the lineage in the transmission of realization from master to student. The transmission of realization is here in the *Masters of the Laṅka* as well, and other sūtras are quoted at least as often as the *Laṅkāvatāra*, but that scripture is still the thread on which the pearls of the lineage masters are strung.

While the two contemporaneous Zen lineage accounts begin with Bodhidharma, the *Masters of the Laṅka* starts with Guṇabhadra, the Indian translator of the *Laṅkāvatāra sūtra*. The fact that the text begins with a translator also shows its debt to the tradition of biographies of eminent monks, which always begin with biographies of translators.[4]

Why the *Laṅkāvatāra sūtra* in particular? It may well be because of the sūtra's concern with explicating a Buddhist model of consciousness and its assertions that all phenomena are mental, and therefore that the transformation of the mind ought to be the focus of practitioners of greater vehicle Buddhism. This would have recommended the sūtra to Chinese monks whose primary activities were practicing and teaching meditation. For a time, the *Laṅkāvatāra* also played an important role in bodhisattva precepts ceremonies. The *Laṅkāvatāra* came to be associated with the influential teacher Shenxiu (607–706); later, as teachers shifted focus to the Perfection of Wisdom literature, this connection with the *Laṅkāvatāra* was sidelined in favor of the *Vajracchedikā*.[5] This is particularly evident in the *Platform Sutra* and other texts associated with the radical teacher Shenhui (684–758), who was forthright in his criticism of Shenxiu. Thus the *Masters of the Laṅka* looks like a transitional work in the emergence of Zen lineage writing.

The placement of Bodhidharma second in *Masters of the Laṅka* was not widely accepted. Indeed, Jingjue was attacked specifically for this in the *Record of the Dharma Jewel through the Generations:*

> He falsely alleged that the Trepiṭaka Guṇabhadra was the first patriarch. I do not know his source, but he deluded and confused later students by saying Guṇabhadra was the Patriarchal Master Dharma's master. Guṇabhadra was from the first a scripture-translating Trepiṭaka, a student of the Lesser Vehicle, not a Chan Master. He translated the *Laṅkā-sūtra* in four fascicles, but he did not give an explanation of the *Laṅkā-sūtra* or transmit it to the Patriarchal Master Dharma. . . . When this Master Jingjue falsely alleged that Guṇabhadra was the first patriarch he profoundly confused the study of the Dharma.[6]

Though it clearly had its detractors, the *Masters of the Laṅka* is not all that remains of the *Laṅkāvatāra* lineage in Zen. A text called *Verses on the Siddhaṃ according to the Zen Gate of the Laṅkāvatāra* has survived among the Chinese Dunhuang manuscripts. The text is a series of verses on Zen practice, including a practice known as "observing the mind" that is well represented elsewhere in the Chinese and Tibetan Zen manuscripts (see chapter 7).[7] Thus the *Laṅkāvatāra* lineage transmitted a complex of practices, and the *Masters of the Laṅka* places those practices in the context of a lineage.

LINEAGE AS PRACTICE

Recent scholarship on Zen lineage histories such as the *Masters of the Laṅka* has been critical to the point of hostility. The historical inaccuracy of the texts and the way they were constructed to fit the facts to the needs of a particular lineage have led some to see in them nothing more than hidden agendas of self-promotion, or at least the promotion of the lineage. There is surely some truth in this. Each lineage account is constructed to present itself as genuine and worthy, sometimes to the detriment of other lineages. In most cases, no doubt, the need for monks to attract patrons informed the production of these lineage accounts. However, this view of the texts and those who used them is limited by its failure to take practice into account.

The actual biographical lineage in the *Masters of the Lanka* is a skeleton fleshed out by the teachings attributed to the masters and supporting quotations from Buddhist scripture. As biography, the text is meager, with only brief accounts of how the lineage masters received and practiced the teachings. Even the accounts of miraculous activities that give the *Record of the Transmission of the Dharma Jewel* its flavor are largely missing. What we have instead is a fairly sober anthology. As we saw in the previous section, the Lankāvatāra school transmitted a complex of Zen practices. If we are aware of this, it becomes evident that *Masters of the Lanka* mainly comprises teachings and quotations that support and contextualize those practices.

An exception to the tendency to view lineage accounts as primarily political in function is the work of John McRae that links them explicitly with practices, arguing that "it is not only the Zen school's self-understanding of its own religious history, but the religious practice of Zen itself that is fundamentally genealogical."[8] Though McRae's assertion in the same passage that the genealogical nature of Zen is distinct from any other Buddhist tradition may be overstated (we see the central importance of lineage accounts and the master-disciple relationship in many forms of Tibetan Buddhism), his insistence on seeing lineage as a form of practice is surely right. The *Masters of the Lanka* validates the practices it describes with a lineage that goes back to India and is linked to a scripture recording the words of the Buddha. It would thus be vital to a teacher attempting to impress students and patrons with the authority and proven effectiveness of this practice as against those of other teachers. In the discourses of the masters and the scriptural quotations that make up most of the text, the *Masters of the Lanka* would also have provided source material for teachers, whether in the context of individual instruction or sermons to groups.

We saw in the previous chapter that the text preceding the *Masters of the Lanka* in the manuscript IOL Tib J 710 contains advice for meditation teachers on the relationship between teachers and students. That text and the present one are linked by their physical presence in the same manuscript, where they are written in the same handwriting; they are also linked by the theme of teachers and students. Placing both texts in dialogue with each other, and considering the manuscript containing them as belonging to a teacher of meditation in the Zen style, we can see how the *Masters of the Lanka* would offer such a teacher an idealized model of the teacher-student relationship. The text powerfully communicates the image of a single realized master passing on his realization, like water poured from one vase to another, or a flame passed from one lamp to another, complementing the more practical advice on that relationship in the text preceding it.

THE TIBETAN VERSION

The Tibetan translation of the *Masters of the Lanka* differs from the Chinese in interesting ways. It is much shorter than the Chinese version, lacking the preface by the author Jingjue, some teachings attributed to Gunabhadra and Bodhidharma, and the entire second half of the lineage.[9] This suggests that the text was supplemented over time. Since Jingjue's authorship is only stated in the preface, it is possible that he was not the author of the basic text that we have in Tibetan translation but later expanded on it and made it his own. There would be nothing untoward about this in a manuscript culture in which there is no concept of intellectual copyright and only a loose conception of individual authorship.[10]

The style of the Tibetan translation of the *Masters of the Lanka* is quite different from most translated Tibetan literature, whether from Sanskrit or Chinese. For example, a common Sanskrit Buddhist term like *pratītyasamutpāda* ("dependent origination") is rendered in Tibetan as *rkyen las gyo ba* rather than the usual *rten cing 'brel ba*. This suggests that the text was translated before the standardization of the Tibetan translation language in the second decade of the ninth century. Another possibility was suggested by Rolf Stein: that the Tibetans used different translation languages for Sanskrit and Chinese. But this is dubious; the Dunhuang translator Chödrup, who worked in the mid-ninth century, did not use a different vocabulary than that used for translation from Indian texts. In addition, *Masters of the Lanka* has some genuinely old

Tibetan orthography, like *rma* instead of *dmar* for "red" and *dard pa* for "youth." These and other archaic words found in the text strongly indicate that the *Masters of the Laṅka* was translated into Tibetan during the early phase of translation in the late eighth century or early ninth century.[11]

The Tibetan version of the *Masters of the Laṅka* contains brief lives and longer explications of the teachings of five masters of meditation: Guṇabhadra, Bodhidharma, Huike, Sengcan, and Daoxin. The first section begins with the experience of Guṇabhadra's arriving in China and finding it wanting as a place for teaching the greater vehicle compared to his homeland in India. In this passage, China is characterized as a place where there is confusion regarding the Buddhist dharma, where many are devoted to harmful practices involving gods and spirits, magical spells, and prognostications. This characterization of China sets the scene for the transformation that is to be wrought by Guṇabhadra and his lineage.

This scene setting extends to the teachings of Guṇabhadra as well, in which the *Laṅkāvatāra* is quoted, along with other sūtras. He begins by telling his Chinese audience how the dharma that he teaches is secret in India, how it is not suitable for ordinary people, but only those of great merit, and how it is passed on only from a single teacher to a single student, in a relationship like that of a father and a son. This father-son model is, of course, also the structure of the *Masters of the Laṅka* itself. Guṇabhadra goes on to discuss the mental state that his teachings reveal, the "mind at ease," which has four successive levels. The highest level is that of sameness, or nonduality, in which there is no difference between actions that are virtuous and those that are not, or between buddhas and ordinary sentient beings. From this position, Guṇabhadra criticizes scholasticism, using metaphors for the immanence of the enlightened state including the sun's appearing from behind the clouds and a mirror's being wiped clean.

Next in the lineage, Bodhidharma is explicitly described as a student of Guṇabhadra, and his first quoted words are a recommendation of the *Laṅkāvatāra*, which he calls "the grandfather of practices." The teaching specific to Bodhidharma is summarized as threefold: developing a mind at ease by gazing at a wall, developing one's practice through the four practices, and being harmonious by avoiding the urge to humiliate and offend others. By invoking the mind at ease and linking it to Bodhidharma's "wall gazing," the *Masters of the Laṅka* creates a segue from the teachings of one master to the next. The rest of the section on Bodhidharma is a version of the only surviving text now considered to come from Bodhidharma himself: *The Two Entrances and Four Practices*.

The success of *The Two Entrances and Four Practices* was probably due to the way it managed to combine an immanent, nondual ethos (which it calls "the entrance of the universal principle") with prosaic instructions on how to practice ("the entrance of practice"). This would have made it a useful pedagogical aid for teachers imparting the Zen ethos while also encouraging students to cultivate meditation, the kind of teachers and students that the previous text in IOL Tib J 710 addresses. Very briefly, the universal principle is the true nature of experience, cultivated through gazing at a wall. The four practices are (i) contemplating the fact that one's present misfortunes are due to one's previous negative actions extending back into previous lives; (ii) contemplating the fact that good things like praise and fame are based on ephemeral causes and conditions and do not last; (iii) giving up effort as the way to avoid the cycle of suffering; and (iv) acting in accord with the universal principle. This final practice makes it clear that the universal principle is not separate from practice but expressed through it.

The sections on the following three Chinese masters in *Masters of the Laṅka* are less coherent, having the character of an anthology of quotations. Themes that were brought up earlier—the immanent presence of the enlightened mind, the nonduality of conventional dichotomies, the uselessness of learning—are repeated at more length. Another theme in meditation practice emerges in the final section of the Tibetan version, which is on the master Daoxin. This is the "single practice concentration." Though this term was used to describe different approaches to practice in the works of different Zen masters, it has the general significance of abandoning a plethora of meditation practices for a single practice that is sufficient in itself.[12] Here it is described as a practice of sitting in front of a real or visualized image of the Buddha:

> If you want to enter the single practice concentration, reside in solitude, and abandon intellectual disturbances. Letting go of

forms and features, think only of the features of a single buddha. Facing the buddha, sit up straight in the way that he does. If you connect your mind with the features of the single buddha in front of you, then within your mind you will be able to see all the buddhas of the past and future.

And as we saw in the previous text in IOL Tib J 710, the tension between the rhetoric of the single practice and the practicalities of actually teaching meditation to students of various personalities made it necessary to justify the teaching of a variety of practices while preserving the ethos of the single practice. Again, we can see how the scribe who copied these two texts into the same manuscript was bringing together texts about practices and how to teach them. We can also see how a lineage text like the *Masters of the Laṅka* could work as a sourcebook for teaching and practice.

Record of the Masters and Students of the Laṅka

---

1. GUṆABHADRA

We begin with the teachings of Guṇabhadra. During the reign of the Song emperors, the Tripitaka Master Guṇabhadra lived in the country of Madhya in India. He understood the scholarship of the greater vehicle, and was known as Master Mahāyāna. In the period known as Yuanjia (424–53), he traveled in a great ship for one year, before arriving in Guangzhou. Emperor Song Taizu received him at Danyang jun.[13]

After he had translated the *Dharma Book of Laṅka,* the sons and queens of the emperor, those who had gone forth from their homes and those who had not, all asked him to begin teaching meditation. But he did not know the language of China's Central Plain and was downhearted. Then, at night, he dreamed that his head was cut off with a sword and had a change of heart. Thus he began to teach meditation. The Master of the Three Dharmas said:

> For those who live in this Eastern country, the dharma is not a way of life. Because it is not, some of you fall into the dharmas of the lesser vehicle and the two vehicles, some fall into the ninety-five dharmas of the heretics, and some fall into the path of gods and spirits, scrutinizing the good or bad prognostications for all people.

He said:

> This is what I see from within meditation: there is this great malevolent influence of affliction. I am sunk in this malevolent

influence, and others are too. I feel sorry for those who are like this, spending a long time on the path of gods and spirits, a long time afflicted within saṃsāra, without attaining liberation. Some fall into the dharma of magical spells, controlling gods and spirits, and making predictions about the future for others. They are all like this. Vulgar, ordinary people, because they are blind and corrupt, do not understand this marvelous dharma.

After he had subdued everyone in this way, they offered support and pledged allegiance. He said:

Hold on to this as the ultimate dharma. Do not study the dharma of the existence of gods, spirits, ghosts, and demons; this is the cause of suffering. In my country of Madhya, the secret dharma that is correct and righteous is not discussed. There are a select few who have causal connections and mature faculties, and if they meet a wise man on the road, the teachings will be bestowed upon them. For those without mature faculties, there will be no one-to-one teaching from father to son. So what need is there even to speak of those whose minds are full of doubt?

In the *Dharma Book of Laṅka* it says: "The mind of the buddha is the best part of oneself. My dharma teaching will remain in a mind that is without agitation."[14] This dharma is superior to the three vehicles, passing beyond them. It transcends the ten grounds. Thus it is the site of the result of ultimate buddhahood. Unquestionably, it is suitable to know this for oneself with a capable mind, but it is not suitable for giving to others who are inferior. Those who are without thoughts should understand it correctly. Those who are without recollection will have a body that is at ease. Those who remain without moving from seclusion preserve that which is fundamental and turn toward that which is correct.

My dharma is secret and precious. It is not suitable to be communicated by ordinary fools with superficial understanding. On the other hand, people who have gathered merit are certainly capable of receiving and practicing it. Those who do not understand it are a hundred out of a hundred. Those who do understand it are one out of a hundred. Those who want to be a buddha should first have a mind that is at ease. If they do not have a mind at ease, then even virtue is not virtuous, so what need is there to speak of negative thoughts? If mind is at ease and unmoving, then there is no difference between the duality of good and bad. The *Gandhavyūha sūtra* says: "Phenomena are not seen by phenomena; phenomena are not known by phenomena."

Since coming to this country, I have not seen anybody practicing the dharma path, so what need is there to speak of those who do not rest in a mind at ease? If I occasionally see the odd person practicing religious activities, they are not in accord with the dharma path. Some do it so that others will hear of their reputation. Some do it for money for their livelihood. Some do it for their master or themselves. Their minds are full of envy. How is that? To act out of envy means that when one sees someone who is not opposed to the dharma path practicing it, going directly to the universal principle, understanding it and putting it into practice, so that those who see this offer their support and pledge allegiance and he obtains a little money to support himself, then one feels envy, one's mental state is angry and unhappy, and one thinks, "I am better than him" and clings to this assertion. The name of this is "envy."

Even with understanding and knowledge and diligently practicing day and night, cutting off sorrow and clearing away obstacles and impediments, clouds and obstructions will move across the dharma path, one after another. The name for this is "practicing the dharma" but it is not the mind at ease. Some teach the six perfections and the dharma and practice meditation, some attain the second and third levels of meditation, all the while energetically practicing afflicted activities, and all this without end. The name for this is "virtue," but it is not what we call dharma practice.[15] A monk who waters the fields of the dharma path and does not grow the seeds of discriminating awareness within it—this is dharma practice.

As for "mind at ease," in brief, there are four types: (i) The mind that is contrary to the universal principle, which is generally the mind of an ordinary person. (ii) The mind that tends toward the universal principle and seeks nirvāṇa out of disillusionment with saṃsāra; tending toward emptiness and stillness, this is known as "the mind of the hearers." (iii) The mind that tends toward the universal principle, cutting through obscuration and engaging with the universal principle; yet, since this is a way of being (*sattva*) that is skilled in ordinary mental states, it is not the mind of enlightenment (*bodhicitta*). (iv) The mind of sameness: not mistaking the inner, not mistaking the outer, it is in accord with the universal principle of sameness. This is the mind of a buddha. Not seeing the difference between ordinary and marvelous, saṃsāra and nirvāṇa, means and wisdom, the universal principle and the meaning of nonduality arise simultaneously. The duality of habitual mental states and purity is also oneness. Even buddhas and sentient beings are the same, essentially one. The name for this pure essence is "the mind of sameness."

In the *Dharma Book of Laṅka* it says: "All things are without nirvāṇa. Buddhas are beyond nirvāṇa. They are free from the experience of experience, free from the duality of existence and nonexistence." The dharma path of the greater vehicle does not deviate from the fundamental. It is especially pure. It comes from the fundamental and is not obtained through causation. It is like the way the light of the sun is obscured by drifting clouds: when the clouds disperse, the sun appears. What is the use of varied and extensive learning? If one sees or hears written letters or spoken words as manifold as atoms or grains of sand, one will turn back toward the path of saṃsāra. People who practice verbal explanations and scribbled words as the dharma path are attached to money and livelihood. They ruin themselves and ruin others. They are not virtuous friends.

It is like wiping a mirror: once the stains are removed, the mirror is bright and pure. Thus, all phenomena are fundamentally not to be acted upon. The *Dharma Book* says: "The actions of the buddhas do not exist, nor does the liberation of sentient beings by buddhas." Sentient beings impose firm distinctions and think that buddhas save sentient beings. If that thought prevents them from understanding nonactivity, they will lack stability. If they do understand, then they will perceive it directly. The great practice that comes from this situation is vastly pervasive. It is not accepted or grasped. It is called "practicing the great dharma path." It is without the duality of oneself and others. All practices, all rituals and lineages are without past or future, and without an in-between. This is what we call "the greater vehicle."

Having no inner or outer attachment: this ultimate equanimity is known as the great relinquishing and is the perfection of giving. Equanimity toward good and evil, not accepting that duality, is the perfection of morality. Not acting upon mental objects and equanimity toward enemies and friends is the perfection of patience. Practicing like the Sage himself is the perfection of energy. Having no duality between movement and nonmovement is the perfection of meditation. Supreme nonmovement resulting in nonperception is the perfection of wisdom. The name for this kind of understanding is "the greater vehicle."

Those who seek the greater vehicle without having a mind at ease are certain to go astray. The *Dharma Book of the Great Series* says: "The five eyes of the buddhas see all phenomena and the minds of sentient beings, yet ultimately they do not observe anything." The *Gandhavyūha sūtra* says: "If you do not see, you have the power of original sight." The *Sutra of Altruism* says: "It cannot be seen with the eyes. It cannot be known through the ears, nose, tongue, body, ego, or consciousness. It is the sight and hearing and perception and understanding of the tathāgatas. If one has the power to see and hear and perceive and understand in this way, the name for this is direct seeing and understanding."

The *Sutra of Meditation* says: "Bats and owls see nothing during the day but at night they can see objects. Despite this knowledge, it is false thinking that comes from error. How is that so? When bats and owls are in what is darkness for others, they see it as light. And ordinary people see what is light for others as darkness. This is thoroughly false thinking, coming from error. Some, obscured by karma, do not see the correct dharma. And thus, whether in the light or the darkness, they do not have stability. If you understand this, you will not be pierced by the deception and disturbance of error and will enter the pure and permanent happiness of the tathāgatas."

The Great Master said:

This is taught in the *Laṅka Sutra:* "How does one cleanse the mind? Do not think it is mind that is false. Do not think that falsity is the mind. Dissolving other thoughts, think of the buddha. Dissolving other thoughts, think of wisdom. If you constantly think like this, this is emptiness and no-mind, this is fundamental emptiness, this is pure awareness."

Once he also said:

Once received, this will never decline. It is constantly unwavering. This is what was taught by the Buddha.[16]

2. BODHIDHARMA

The Master of the Three Dharmas, Bodhidharma, taught during the Wei period. Bodhidharma studied with Guṇabhadra. The Meditation Master Dharma took sincere pleasure in the greater vehicle. He traveled by sea to Luoyang and Moung Song. The two monks Daoyu and Huike both served him faithfully for five years, before he assessed them in a single day and taught them the four basic practices, saying:

If you practice according to the grandfather of practices, the four-fascicle *Dharma Book of Laṅka,* you will be naturally liberated from saṃsāra.

What follows is drawn from the *Teachings of Realized Monks* and is also found in the preface to the *Four Practices in the Dharma of the Greater Vehicle.* This Dharma Master lived in a country in the south of

India, which lies to the West. He was the third son of an Indian king. His intellect was vast and clear, and he comprehended everything he studied. Since his mind was merged with the greater vehicle, he exchanged his gray robes for dharma robes. Always mindful of the lineage of saints, his disciplined mind was empty and unmoving. Since he comprehended all worldly things, he skillfully transcended the worldly things that manifest both internally and externally.

In his kindness, he taught the foolish people of the borderlands, crossing the wide ocean to bring the teachings from the lineage of the dharma of direct meaning to China. Among those noble people who had experienced the unmoving disciplined mind, there were none who did not believe him and pledge their allegiance. On the other hand, those who accepted forms and were attached to sights wanted to humiliate and overpower him.

At this time, there were two monks, called Daoyu and Huike, who, though only young, had intellects vast and true. Having had the good fortune to meet the Dharma Master, they served him faithfully for many years. After they had been asking him for many months, the master, out of the authenticity of his mind and with unique compassion, taught them the dharma path:

> How do we have a mind at ease? How do we develop our practice? How are we to be in harmony with everything? What is the method for these things? It is the dharma of the mind at ease, found in the greater vehicle, when practiced without confusion or error. The mind that I speak of is that which gazes at the surface of a wall. The development of practice that I speak of is the four practices. The harmony with everything that I speak of is to avoid the urge to humiliate and offend.

These axioms are a very brief version of his teachings; a more detailed account is given immediately below:

> There are many gates through which one can enter the dharma path, as taught in the sūtras, but essentially there are only two. The first is for entering the universal principle, and the second

is for entering the practice. This is a personal teaching on entering the universal principle. The universal principle is experience, and if one holds the deep belief that an ordinary mind and that of a perfect saint are essentially the same, it will be evident without any possibility of being covered up by the merest speck of falsity. To give up false thinking is to turn toward what is right and rest in what is pure. When you gaze at a wall, there is no self, and there is no other. The ordinary person and the saint are one and the same. If you sit resolutely in this way, you will not waver, or follow after speech or words. Your mind will be at one with the perfect universal principle, with no distinction into separate parts, empty, unmoving, and without activity. This is what is called "entering the universal principle."

Entering the practice refers to four practices. Every other practice is included in these meditations. What then are these four practices? They are (i) the practice of retribution for wrongdoing, (ii) the practice that is in accord with causes and conditions, (iii) the practice that is entirely without effort, and (iv) the practice that meets the dharma.

What is "the practice of retribution for wrongdoing"? It is to be done by people who practice the dharma while they are subject to affliction. They should think: "For countless eons I have lost what is fundamental and original, and pursued lesser things. Wandering within the states of existence, agitated by enemies and friends, I have performed countless wrong and harmful actions. Even though I do not act harmfully now, this is a return for the bad things I have done in previous lives. It is the ripening of the fruit of suffering and not something given to me by gods or humans." Thus they will increase their mental endurance and be without anger. As the *Dharma Book* says: "Even though I encounter suffering, I do not cling to unhappiness. Why? Because I know and understand the basic universal principle." When one moves toward that state of mind and is in harmony with the universal principle, angry thoughts do not occur, and one yearns for the dharma path. This is the practice of retribution for wrongdoing.

Second, "the practice that corresponds to causes and conditions." As sentient beings have no self, they are always being transformed by causes and conditions. Happiness and suffering alike come from our causal actions. If I obtain praise and fame in this life, it is due to causes from my previous lives. But once these payments come to an end, they will be gone, so what is there to rejoice about? Gain and loss are nothing more than repayments. When one's mind neither augments nor diminishes this, then if the winds of rejoicing stir, one's intellect stays in accord with the dharma path. Being like this is what we teach as the practice that corresponds to causes and conditions.

Third, "the practice that is entirely without effort." The worldly person is always corrupt, his mind craving the five objects of desire. The name for this is "effort." The wise person fully comprehends the perfect universal principle, and henceforth his mind is at ease. Because he does not engage in any intellectual activity whatsoever, his body is like a gift. Because all existents are empty, he is without aspiration or inspiration. Beautiful truths are always associated with the darkness of ignorance. Spending a long time in the three realms is like being in a house on fire. All bodily things are thoroughly afflicted, so who will find ease? Those who truly understand how to find it cease all thoughts of existents and make no effort. The *Dharma Book* says: "The existence of effort is suffused with suffering. Those who make no effort possess the original happiness." Thus it is evident that being without effort is the correct practice of the dharma path.

Fourth, "the practice that agrees with the dharma."[17] This is dharma activity that comes from the universal principle of the pure essence. The perfect forms that embody this universal principle are empty, untainted, without attachment, and without back and forth. The *Dharma Book* says: "The dharma is without sentient beings; it is free from the stains of sentience. The dharma is without self; it is free from the stains of self." If the wise are able to believe and know that the universal principle is like this, then this is practice that agrees with the dharma.

There is no miserliness in the essence of the dharma; it is to renounce and give away body, life, and wealth, without stinginess or miserliness. If you know and comprehend the three emptinesses, you will act without attachment or hesitation. Certainly, if when teaching sentient beings to purify stains, you act without grasping or attachment, then whatever benefits you will also be of benefit to others and you will be fit to adorn the dharma path to enlightenment. This is the perfection of giving, and the other five perfections are the same. When false thinking has been purified, then even when you are practicing the six perfections, you are not practicing anything. This is practice in agreement with the dharma.

These four practices were taught by the master of meditation Bodhidharma himself.[18]

3. HUIKE

During the Qi period, it was Huike, a monk from Mount Song, who followed Bodhidharma.[19] When the monk Huike was fourteen years old, he met the master of meditation Bodhidharma. He served him faithfully for six years in Mount Song and Luoyang. Having thoroughly grasped the accomplishment of the greater vehicle, he fathomed the depth of the universal principle. The following is from his brief teaching on practicing the dharma path:

> The precious dharma is perceived directly in the mind and turns you toward what is right. The *Dharma Book of Laṅka* says: "The emptiness of the Buddha and one's own examination of the unmoving are beyond birth and death. This is called being purified of the clinging to the difference between the present time and the original time." If you ask whether, out of all the buddhas of the ten directions, there is a single one who achieved buddhahood without it being due to meditation, there is absolutely not.
>
> From the *Daśabhūmika sūtra:* "Within the body of a sentient being, there is the vajra essence of buddhahood. It is like the

sun disk, pure from the beginning, expansive, vast and without limits. Because it is covered up and blocked by the heavy clouds of the five aggregates, sentient beings do not see it. When they meet the wind of insight, the heavy clouds of the five skandhas are cleared away, and once they are gone, the essence of buddha shines everywhere, a vivid and pure presence."

From the *Avataṃsaka sūtra:* "Expansive and vast, it is like the realm of reality. Limitless, it is like emptiness. Yet it is also like the light of a lamp inside a vase, unable to shine out." Or again it is like when clouds simultaneously appear from all eight directions, darkening all under the sky, and even the light of the sun cannot shine. At that time, the sunlight has not gone; it is covered and blocked by the clouds and not seen by sentient beings. Then when the clouds part and are cleared away, the sunlight shines everywhere, radiantly pure and unobscured. This purity is present in sentient beings. The light of insight is like this: heavy clouds of false thoughts about the objects of desire and confused unhappiness about everything that is seen cover up the path of the saints, so that it cannot manifest. Thus, if false thoughts do not arise and you sit without moving, the sun of great insight will shine on its own. This is like the unmoving perfection of the sage.

A worldly book says that ice comes from water, yet ice can block water, and when the ice melts, the water is set free. When you drive out false thought, that is perfect purity. When a person who is a student looks for the dharma path through words from books and spoken phrases, he is like a lamp in the wind: it cannot dispel the darkness, and its flame cannot burn. But if he sits in purity doing nothing, then he will realize his mind on his own. He is like a lamp inside a house: it dispels the darkness, and its light distinguishes one thing from another.

Thus, when sentient beings are aware of the radiant purity of mind, they will be constantly merged with meditation. The blockages at the six gates will all flow, without being caught in the winds of error. Then the lamp of insight will be radiantly pure and will distinguish one thing from another. Thus buddhahood will be accomplished of itself, and the aspirations of your previous practice will be fully realized. Henceforth, you do not see the states of existence. For one who has attained the body of the dharma in this way, all sentient beings, as numerous as dust motes, are no more than one. For the person who is like this, ten billion eons are no more than a moment.

If you cannot generate heroism, diligence, and aspiration, then countless eons will pass, and even if you meet buddhas as numerous as dust motes, they will not be able to do anything. This is because it is sentient beings who save themselves through becoming conscious of their own minds. Sentient beings are not saved by buddhas. If it was buddhas who saved sentient beings, then since in the past we have met buddhas as numerous as dust motes, we should have become buddhas by now. So, if you are not capable of acting out of a resolute mind-set, then you will not understand this from the inside. Though able to explain it with your mouth, you will not be able to practice it with your mind. The *Dharma Book* says: "One who teaches emptiness while remaining within worldly practices is imitating the ultimate path and will not be liberated from birth."

The essence of buddhahood is like the sun in a clear sky, and like the fire that is within wood. Within the body of sentient beings there exists the lamp of the essence of buddhahood. The name for this is "the mirror of wisdom." The mirror of great wisdom outshines the sun and moon, is pure inside and out, and is without boundaries. It is like perfect gold: when gold is refined, the impurities are destroyed, yet the gold is undamaged. Likewise for sentient beings, though the forms of birth and death are exhausted and destroyed, the dharma body is unharmed. Or again, though a clay pot may be smashed, the minute particles are unharmed. Or again, though the waves become still, the nature of water is unharmed.

This is the meaning of sitting in meditation, and it must be verified for oneself. Destroy the mind that looks for the universal principle in books of written dharma, and strive for the accomplishment of buddhahood. There is not one person in ten thousand who does this. It is said in an ancient book that a picture of a pastry is not capable of assuaging hunger. Talking about eating is of no benefit to a guest. Though you may cut off leaf buds, they just come back stronger. The *Avataṃsaka sūtra* says, "It is like a poor man who spends his days and nights counting other people's precious wealth, without possessing even a few coins of his own." Thus it is for somebody who is very learned but does not practice the dharma path.

If you want to read, then look for a moment and quickly put it away. If you get rid of the book but do not sit, this is still like learning from words in books. It is like looking for ice in boiling water, or looking for snow in a stream. The buddhas teach of some things, and of others they do not teach. They do not teach the inner character of the perfection of phenomena, nor do they not teach it. If you understand the truth of one thing, then wherever one goes, ten thousand will follow. As it says in the *Saddharmapuṇḍarīka sūtra:* "Not true, or false. Not the same, or different."

The great teacher said:

When I teach this perfect dharma, I teach it as the truth in which everything is perfect. This truth is like the universal principle; they are not distinct. Polluted from the beginning, we call a jewel a pebble. If I am able to experience it myself, then it is a perfect jewel. Ignorance is the same as insight; they are not distinct. It is clear that all phenomena are in accord with this. Out of compassion for those who see things dualistically, I have taught in these words, written this book.

He also said:

When my mind was stirred for the first time, I cut off one of my arms. From early dusk till midnight I stood in the snow, unaware of the snow rising past my knees. That is how I sought the unsurpassable dharma path. From the *Avataṃsaka sūtra:*

"When you rest in genuine experience from the east, concentration rises in the west. When you rest in genuine experience from the west, concentration rises in the east. If you rest in the genuine experience of the faculty of sight, concentration rises within the phenomena of color. The phenomena of color are directly given. This is beyond thought and cannot be understood by any god or man. When you rest in the genuine experience of the phenomena of color, then discipline arises from the eye, and mind is undisturbed. If you examine the eye, it is found to be unarisen, it is without an inherent nature, empty, unmoving, unmoving, completely unmoving. It is the same with the ear, nose, tongue, body, and all the way up to the intellect. It is the same for a boy, a youth, a father or mother, for a monk or nun, for a hearer, solitary buddha, or bodhisattva, for the six sense faculties, and everything else. They are all connected to each other, without attachment. When all phenomena, a single body or countless bodies, move in a single act, then everything is thus: the body of dharma, the potent universal principle."[20]

4. SENGCAN

During the Sui period, it was the meditation master Sengcan of Mount Sikong in Shuzhou who followed Huike. According to the *Book of Sayings of Learned Monks,* the one called Sengcan followed Huike and lived on Mount Sikong. He rested in the truth, without stirring. He had no interest in memorizing writings from books and taught the dharma secretly on a one-to-one basis. His sole disciple was the monk Daoxin, who acted as Sengcan's servant. Over twelve years they developed a connection akin to pouring from one vessel into another, or lighting one lamp from another. Sengcan said, "Daoxin has seen directly the state that is the very essence of buddhahood." He said to Daoxin:

The *Book of the Lotus of the Dharma* says: "The truth is found only in the greater vehicle. The two other vehicles are not correct." Thus the dharma path of the saints is very profound and cannot be completed by verbal expressions. The noble body of the dharma does not move from emptiness and cannot be apprehended by sight or hearing. Thus explanations from written books and spoken words are completely without benefit. The *Laṅka*, the sūtra that is the universal principle of a mind at ease in the special greater vehicle that distinguishes truth from error, says "the dharma path of the saints is silence, never taught in words."

The great master said:

Everyone else believes that to practice precious meditation at the end is a great miracle, but I shall now transform birth and death while standing.

After he had said this, he seized a tree branch with his hand and ceased breathing. Afterward, he was taken to a temple on Mount Huangong.[21] There a luminous body of the saint manifested, and he returned once again to his own house. Everyone praised him to each other. He always used to say:

Praise to the one, from the one. The one is vast and profound. It is mixed with the many, that is, all the objects in existence. There is a difference between the perfect and the ordinary, but they are alike in the sūtras. Ordinary people and saints are different, but they are in accord on the path. When you try to define an end point, it is limitless, with no end to be found. There is no beginning. There is no end. Insight and distortion are one and the same. Pollution and purity, the two things that come from them, are the same. The same as emptiness, not going anywhere, in accord with everything that exists between the earth and the sky. Perfect gold is the same as the bracelets and other things that it is turned into. An expanse of water is not diminished by the ice that solidifies within it.

This teaching is saying that the illumination of the universal principle is not mixed with darkness. This is why he speaks of ends and limits.

The essence of perfection is not a substance that can be made. It does not begin, or decline at the end. Thus what are called "illumination" and "darkness" are not two different gates. Good and evil are exhausted in the dharma of the single form. Thus there is no movement that is not empty, no difference that is not in accord. This is like the sameness of water and waves. The vessel made from gold is not nongold. The waves are not nonwater.

> When one investigates conditioned arising, there is no obstruction. Thinking about the nature of all existents, it is difficult to trust them. They are like the polished jewels on a jeweled palace. Suspended from a crystal platform, they are mutually distinguished, each entered into the form of the other. When red and purple separate, they contaminate each other. Substances are not obstructed by "what belongs to me" and "what belongs to others." Meaning is not impeded by the erroneous and the correct. The phenomena of the great thousandfold universe are like the sky. In an instant, one sees all the meanings of the three times. Because there are few who believe these words, I have borrowed Indra's net to clear away doubts. Although the all-seeing eye can see this, the doubting mind does not know it.

This teaching is the secret and precious direct showing of conditioned arising. In the universe of phenomena that is Indra's net, everything comes from one. Forms are not distinct, nor are they one and the same. Thus, if forms are false, their arising is dependent on perfection. If one understands the universal principle of perfection, then forms are entirely unobstructed. Though great and small are not distinct, they are like a mirror and the reflections that appear in it. The form and its features are distinguished as "mutually entering the one into the other." Even with forms of different colors, all come from one, and one comes from all. Conditioned arising is unobstructed.

> In the universal principle, the great thousandfold universe abides in a tiny atom without constraint, and there is room for the great length of the three times to be encompassed in a single

moment. If you see this immensity yourself, you can see through a golden wall without being blocked; you can pass through a stone cliff without experiencing obstruction. This is how saintly people attain the universal principle and practice accomplishment. If the universal principle did not make it possible, the saints would not have such powers. If you know this, then the universal principle is also liberation, and obstruction is the result of intellectual impediments. The wisdom of the mental eye is able to know the truth of perfection. When the monkey is placed in iron chains, the wild mind is disciplined. When the snake enters a tube, his curves become straight. If you are crossing a great sea, use the ship of the dharma. If you need to illuminate the darkness, use the lamp of insight.

In this teaching, the monkey placed in chains is a metaphor for the application of mental discipline. The snake placed in a tube is a metaphor for stopping mental disturbance. In *Liberation through Insight,* it says, "The nature of the snake's movement is curved, but when placed in a tube it is straight." This is like the application of the mind through contemplation. The third chapter, on the three bodies, in the *Dharma Book of Golden Radiance* says, "Though there are three names for the Buddha, there are not three essences."

5. DAOXIN

During the period of the Chinese emperor Li, the meditation master Daoxin of Mount Shuangfeng in Jizhou followed the meditation master Sengcan. The meditation master Daoxin studied the gate to meditation, opened it, and disseminated it over everything under the sky. He left behind a single book, *The Dharma of Bodhisattva Conduct,* and the precious gate to the dharma methods for entering the path with a mind at ease.

I teach for those who possess the conditions and have mature faculties. This precious dharma of mine is in accord with the *Dharma Book of Laṅka* and is the supreme dharma of all the buddhas. It is also in accord with the teaching on the single practice concentration taught in the *Dharma Book of Insight by Mañjuśrī:* the mind that thinks buddha is buddha. Yet if you express this thought, you are an ordinary person.

In the *Dharma Book of Insight by Mañjuśrī,* it says: "Mañjuśrī said, "Blessed One, what is it that you call the great concentration of the single practice?" The Buddha said, "The causes of all phenomena and the realm of reality are what I call the single practice concentration. The causes of attachment have a single feature and the realm of reality has a single feature, and its name is the single practice concentration. Virtuous men and women! If you want to enter the single practice concentration, then you must first ask about the perfection of insight.

"Once you have trained in this teaching, you will be able to enter the single practice concentration. This is in accord with the realm of reality, which is beyond thought, without obstruction, and without features. Virtuous men and women! If you want to enter the single practice concentration, reside in solitude and abandon intellectual disturbances. Letting go of forms and features, think only of the features of a single buddha. Facing the buddha, sit up straight in the way that he does. If you connect your mind with the features of the single buddha in front of you, then within your mind you will be able to see all the buddhas of the past and future. How is that? The merit of thinking of a single buddha is uncountable and unbounded. It is nondual with the merit of countless buddhas, and it is one with the dharmas of an unthinkable number of buddhas. There is no difference. Everything is this single vehicle. Accomplish the supreme genuine experience, and you will come to possess uncountable merit."

Thus, those who enter the single practice concentration know that there is no distinguishing feature in all the realms of buddhas, which are as numerous as grains of sand. In their bodies and minds, and wherever they lift and set down their feet, it is always on the pure ground of the dharma. Wherever they go and whatever they do is enlightenment. The *Dharma Book of*

Samantabhadra's Investigation says, "The whole ocean of karmic obscuration arises from false thinking. If you want to repent of this, sit up straight and think of the true form." The name for this is "the first repentance," and it purifies the mind of the three poisons, the mind of the secondary poisons, the mind that conceptualizes experience, and the mind that searches for buddhahood. When mind is joined on to mind, there is nothing but a quiet and empty space.

The *Dharma Book of the Great Series* says, "Not thinking of anything is what we call thinking of the Buddha. Another name for this is nonmind." Thinking of the Buddha is what we call nonmind. If you are free from mind, there is no buddha apart from this. If you are free from buddha, there is no mind apart from this. Thinking of the Buddha is itself thinking of the mind. Seeking the mind is itself seeking the Buddha. How is that? In the mind, consciousness is formless. In the Buddha, appearance is formless.[22]

ENCOUNTER AND EMPTINESS

ENCOUNTER DIALOGUES

Dialogues between an aspiring student and an enlightened master, in which the master's answer subverts the student's assumptions implicit in the question, are probably the best-known form of Zen literature. Here is one of out hundreds of examples, attributed to the eighth-century master Shitou:

> A monk asked Shitou, "Why did the First Ancestor come from the West? Shitou said, "Ask the temple pillar." The monk said, "I don't understand." Shitou said, "I don't understand either."[1]

These dialogues often involve apparent non sequiturs, hostile or combative answers, and unexpected physical actions like slapping or chasing the student. Though they are vital to the later Zen tradition, they are not at all characteristic of either Tibetan or Chinese Zen as we find it in the Dunhuang manuscripts. The first major collection of such dialogues, the *Anthology of the Patriarchal Hall* (*Zutang ji*), appeared in China in 952, and the classic source for placing these dialogues in the Zen lineage history is the *Record of the Transmission of the Lamp* (*Jingde chuandeng lu*), which appeared in 1004. Neither of these is found in the Dunhuang library cave, and the Zen manuscripts in Chinese and Tibetan display no awareness of the fully developed tradition of what John McRae has termed "encounter dialogues." The Dunhuang manuscripts do however contain several texts that show the antecedents to this classic genre of

Zen literature. These manuscripts help us to see encounter dialogues as performative and conventionalized, rather than as straightforward historical records of what such and such a master said to one of his students.[2]

As we have already seen in chapter 1, the literary form of questions and answers could be used in the context of Zen initiation ceremonies, as a means of orienting those new to Zen practice and ethos to its position, and legitimacy, in the Buddhist tradition. This concern with answering all potential objections is also to be seen in the question and answer text in chapter 6. The text translated here, *A Summary of the Practice of the Instantaneous Approach,* is somewhat different. It takes a more confident stance, developing an image of a Zen master comfortable in the practical application of the emptiness of all conceptual formulations. Still, it is not quite the classical form of encounter dialogue, as neither master nor student is named. What we have instead is a generally applicable paradigm that shows a model of an idealized meditation teacher employing a heuristic method of giving provocative answers to students' questions.[3]

While *A Summary of the Practice of the Instantaneous Approach* and the later encounter dialogues give the impression of being records of spontaneous discussions, there is evidence that they might be better understood as a development of liturgical rituals. A text found in the Chinese Dunhuang manuscripts, the *Five Skillful Means,* is a liturgical ritual in the Zen idiom, which begins with the practitioners taking the vows of a bodhisattva and confessing their transgressions. The main part of the liturgy concerns meditation and its doctrinal context, and it is staged as a conversation between a preceptor and the practitioners. For example:

> The preceptor asks: What do you see?
> Answer: I do not see a single thing.
> Question: When viewing, what things do you view?
> [Answer]: Viewing, no thing is viewed.
>
> The preceptor strikes the wooden [signal-board] and asks:
>   Do you hear the sound?
> [Answer:] We hear.
> [Question:] What is this "hearing" like?

[Answer:] Hearing is motionless.
[Question:] What is the transcendence of thoughts?
[Answer:] The transcendence of thoughts is motionless.[4]

Thus it is possible that the literature of encounter dialogues grew out of these liturgical forms.[5] In any case, even if a dialogue like *A Summary of the Practice of the Instantaneous Approach* was not used as liturgy, it still played some role in practice. When we look at the manuscript in which this text is found, Pelliot tibétain 121, the other texts that the scribe wrote shed some light on its possible use. The dialogue is followed by an explanation of the hierarchy of philosophical views (also translated below), a popular series of verses on meditation practice, an explanation of the "three phrases" of the teacher Wuzhu, and a treatise on various Buddhist concepts, such as the three jewels and ten virtues. These are didactic texts, made for study or teaching. They are written one after the other on a small concertina manuscript, in a rough and ready handwriting style.

It is likely that the scribe was writing quickly and that the manuscript was probably intended for his or her own personal use.[6] What would be the purpose of doing this? Perhaps the contents of this manuscript represent a complex of texts used by a group of teachers and students. Such students might copy, from other sources, particular sequences of texts for their own use in study or recitation. The compact size of Pelliot tibétain 121 also suggests personal rather than ceremonial use. There is no textual indication of the use of the manuscript found in the manuscript itself, but we do have a number of Chinese manuscripts from Dunhuang in which the scribes have explicitly stated that they were lay students copying out texts. Several of these manuscripts include Zen texts.[7]

EMPTINESS AND ZEN

Though the *Laṅkāvatāra sūtra* was an important scriptural source in the early development of Zen, as we saw in the previous chapter, it gradually lost this role as lineages began to make more use of the Perfection of Wisdom literature, especially the *Vajracchedikā sūtra*. Nowhere is this more clear than in the *Platform Sutra* composed (or compiled) by

Shenhui in the eighth century, which extols the virtues of the *Vajracche-dikā*. The *Platform Sūtra* begins with a narrative account of the enlighten-ment of the monk Huineng, whose lineage Shenhui adopted. According to the story, when Huineng was a boy he worked in a marketplace sell-ing wood. One day he heard a customer reciting the *Vajracchedikā* and experienced a sudden clarity of mind. He asked the man where he had learned the sūtra. The man replied that he had been to see the fifth pa-triarch of the Zen school, Hongren, who had told an audience of monks and laypeople that by merely memorizing the *Vajracchedikā* they would see their true natures and become buddhas. So Huineng went to find Hongren, joined his monastery, and ultimately became the sixth patri-arch of the Zen school.

In the Zen initiation ceremony that forms the center of the *Platform Sutra,* Huineng uses the *Vajracchedikā* extensively; this pattern is also found in Pelliot tibétain 116, which as we have seen, contains a complete copy of the *Vajracchedikā*. So why this particular sūtra? Essentially, the *Vajracchedikā* is a dialogue between the Buddha and his disciple Subhuti. Out of this conversation, two main topics emerge. The first is the doc-trine of emptiness. This is characteristic of all Perfection of Wisdom lit-erature, but the *Vajracchedikā* takes a particular approach to it, eschewing argument and analysis and not even using the term "emptiness." Instead the Buddha repeatedly makes contradictory statements, celebrating the virtuous path of a bodhisattva and the qualities of a buddha at the same time as denying that that they exist. This approach is a challenge to du-alistic concepts, and particularly to the conceptualization of Buddhist practice as a prescribed path followed by a result.

The rhetorical negations of the Perfection of Wisdom literature were complemented in the Indian Buddhist tradition by the philosophical treatises of the Madhyamaka or "Middle Way" approach. Beginning with Nāgārjuna in the second century AD, Madhyamaka texts attempted to refute current religio-philosophical views on the existence of entities (*dharma*) found in the Buddhist Abhidharma literature and in various other Indian traditions. According to Madhyamaka, all dharmas are empty (*śūnya*) of independent existence. Nāgārjuna and his followers of-ten used the negative approach of trying to show the inconsistency in the philosophical positions of others, but also taught that dependent arising (*pratītyasamutpāda*), the dependence of all things upon other things for their existence, offers a middle way between the extreme views of eternalism and nihilism. Thus the emptiness of entities is the same thing as their being dependently originated.

While the influence of Madhyamaka on Chinese Zen has been discussed, this influence is even more apparent among the Tibetan Zen manuscripts. For example, a brief text called *A Teaching on the Essence of Contemplation by Master Haklenayaśas* presents Zen as "the instantaneous approach to the Madhyamaka":

> There are many gates to meditation in the greater vehicle. The ultimate among them is the instantaneous approach to the Madhyamaka. The instantaneous approach has no method. One just cultivates the nature of reality in this way: phenomena are mind, and mind is uncreated. In that it is uncreated, it is emptiness. Since it is like the sky, it is not a subject for the six sense faculties. This emptiness is what we call experience. Yet within that experience, there is no such thing as experience. Therefore without remaining in the insights gained from studying, cultivate the essential sameness of all phenomena.[8]

This short text—attributed to the Indian master who came to be counted as the twenty-third in the Indian lineage of Zen patriarchs—offers a practice-based Madhyamaka, where emptiness is understood through two stages, first understanding that all phenomena are mental, and second that the mind is "uncreated"—does not exist in and of itself. This approach to the Madhyamaka was also very popular in the later Tibetan Sakya and Kagyü traditions.[9]

The second text translated below immediately follows *A Summary of the Practice of the Instantaneous Approach* in Pelliot tibétain 121 and is titled *The Meaning of Madhyamaka in the Greater Vehicle*. It sets out a hierarchy of non-Buddhist and Buddhist philosophies, beginning with the non-Buddhist nihilists, followed by non-Buddhist eternalists, who believe in the permanent existence of the self (Skt. *ātman*, Tib. *bdag*) as against the temporary status of the person (Skt. *pudgala*, Tib. *gang zag*). The way the text here plays on the two parts of the Tibetan word (*gang*

= "fullness" and *zag* = "exhaustion") suggests that it was composed in the Tibetan language. The next stage in the hierarchy are the hearers and solitary realizers, both of whom are considered to fall short of greater vehicle aspirations by neglecting the welfare of all sentient beings and attaining a nirvāṇa that is only for their own benefit (though here the solitary realizers are said to benefit beings indirectly after their attainment of nirvāṇa).

After this, the greater vehicle is divided into two main philosophical schools, the Vijñānavāda, or "Way of Consciousness," and the Madhyamaka. The first of these is presented as teaching that all things are merely consciousness and that there are three aspects to all things, the ultimate of which is wisdom. Though the first two aspects are nonexistent, wisdom does exist. This last point is where Madhyamaka attacks on the Vijñānavāda were often directed, and this is represented here.

As for the Madhyamaka, it is divided into the two approaches that were in vogue when Buddhism was established in Tibet in the eighth and ninth centuries: Yoga Madhyamaka and Sautrantika Madhyamaka (the latter meaning "the Madhyamaka of those who follow the sūtras"). Here Yoga Madhyamaka is presented as the same as Vijñānavāda apart from their rejection of an ultimately existing wisdom. The Sautrantika Madhyamaka is presented according to the two levels of truth, relative and ultimate. The relative truth is the appearance of all things in dependence, like magical illusions. The ultimate truth is the negation of all conceptual distinctions: "nondual, free from the four extremes, without birth or cessation, transcending the realm of spoken or written language, without acceptance or rejection, not any kind of substance, not remaining or ceasing, free from subject and object." By placing the Sautrantika Madhyamaka last in the hierarchy, the text implies that this is the ultimate philosophical view.

Interestingly, this places *The Meaning of Madhyamaka in the Greater Vehicle* apart from the approach found in the brief text attributed to Haklenayaśas. Overall, this text is closer to the Tibetan tradition than the Chinese. A very similar discussion of the philosophical hierarchy is found in *Distinguishing the Views,* a text attributed to the eighth-century Tibetan translator Zhang Yeshe De, found in the Tibetan canon as well as in a Dunhuang manuscript. Other canonical texts and manuscripts present similar hierarchies, and in the later Tibetan tradition, the exposition of philosophical views followed the same template, with only minor changes in content.[10]

On the other hand, *The Meaning of Madhyamaka in the Great Vehicle* differs from those others in presenting the hierarchy of philosophical views firmly in the framework of meditation practice. The opening passage sets the context as the cultivation of yoga, emphasizing the primary importance of this practice but warning that even meditators can go astray if they hold an eternalist or nihilist view (Tib. *lta ba,* Skt. *dārṣana*). The final passage affirms the connection between a proper philosophical understanding and successful meditation practice, bringing the text to a close with the words "you sit with the mind in equanimity."

Thus, returning to the context of the manuscript itself, the rapidly executed handwriting and the texts written in Pelliot tibétain 121 suggest that it was written by a student in a lineage of instruction in which meditation practice was central, but accompanied with some doctrinal teaching. The doctrinal side is presented in a concise fashion here (and also in the last text in the manuscript, a collection of various Buddhist enumerations such as the three jewels), such as would be appropriate to a lay student or a novice monk, as an adjunct to meditation.

A Summary of the Practice of
the Instantaneous Approach

Causes and effects are not established entities, nor do they arise by their own nature. They do not abide, nor are they apprehended at any extreme. This is *the ultimate truth.* As for the great vehicle, it is because it is supreme and surpasses the hearers, solitary realizers, and bodhisattvas that it is known as *the great vehicle.* As for *Madhyamaka,* it does not remain at any of the extremes of eternalism and nihilism, or existence and nonexistence. It is not an object of discussion in spoken and written words. The lack of existence is not like the sky; the lack of nonexistence is not like the horns of a rabbit. The lack of existence at the beginning is not taught as nonexistence in the present moment. The Buddha said, "Let experience arise without thinking of anything," but this is only taught to beginners. Lionlike sages endowed with great diligence do not discuss the arising of experience. They abide without conceptualizing any of the four types of activity, wherever they go.

Question: Do you see this finger?

Answer: I see it.

Another question: Are you seeing it now?

Answer: I am seeing it.

Question: If it is possible to see this finger when it exists, how can you see it when it doesn't exist? This is a great marvel!

Answer: The finger comes in and goes out of existence, but is seen continuously. How is this a great marvel? The main point is established by the words of the Buddha: "If one is separated from sight, hearing, experience, and consciousness of phenomena, then how does one see anything? The answer is this: Because the ignorant, hearers, and solitary realizers have inferior views and are attached to features, I teach this separation as a skillful means." If you understand this point, then you will not be separate from seeing, hearing, feeling, or consciousness of phenomena.

   Why shouldn't afflicted emotions be enlightenment? It is like water and ice not being different. Based on the first moment of experience, you know experience in its very essence. When you know experience in its essence, then you instantaneously know the subsequent experiences of all sentient beings. The meaning of perfect experience is said to be that it does not arise even at the beginning. When it comes, where does it come from, and when it goes, where does it go? It is like gold coins sewn inside a poor man's clothing. Even while they are unseen, they are not nonexistent. When they are revealed and seen, it is not that they have been subsequently acquired. Therefore, when you understand the meaning of this, the first moment of experience is subsequent experience, and subsequent experience is not separate from the first.

Question: Do you see form?

Answer: Form does not see me.

Question: Are you really like that?

Answer: I am indeed. I do not conceptualize anything.

Question: What name do you give this?

Answer: Ask me a question!

Question: If you have no perception of form, then how can we
converse with questions and answers? I will ask a question
about the views regarding whether perception exists or does
not exist.

Answer: I see the existence *and* the nonexistence of perception.

Question: How do you see that?

Answer: I do not see the existence of perception, or the
nonexistence of perception.

Question: How are all phenomena pure?[11]

Answer: Neither phenomena nor mind exists. When the
conceptual mind arises, everything is mistaken. If mind is
nonconceptual, all phenomena are perfect.

Question: Can you give a definitive name for phenomena
themselves?

Answer: There is no name for phenomena; what name could be
given?

Question: Is it existent phenomena that have no name, or
nonexistent phenomena?

Answer: I am separate from existent and nonexistent phenomena.

Question: How can you be separate from existent and
nonexistent phenomena?

Answer: Because reality is separate from them all.

A Summary of the Practice of Immediate Entry is complete.

The Meaning of Madhyamaka in
the Greater Vehicle

Those who want to know how to realize the perfect space of reality, the perfection of insight, must first of all rely on the three kinds of insight. With the insights of learning and thinking, they initially resolve the view, and then with the insight of cultivating the sameness of the space of reality, they cultivate the yoga of becoming accustomed to this at all times. But if they have not already resolved the view, then they will fall into apprehension of the four extremes, such as eternalism or nihilism. Apprehension is a fault in the perfection of insight. Where there is a widespread teaching via apprehension, such as the various philosophical views involving apprehension, then a great many forms of existence and nonexistence are enumerated. However, the various heretical views can be summarized as the dyad of eternalism and nihilism.

With the heretics, in the system of Vṛthāsuta, there are no previous or future lives, no virtuous or evil actions, no effects of virtuous or evil actions, no heaven or hell, and no saṃsāra or nirvāṇa.[12] This body merely arises adventitiously from the causes and conditions of one's father and mother. In this life, after having experienced happiness and suffering, after dying everything ceases. A fire that has exhausted its fuel and a fire that has died out do not exist at all. That is their view.

In the system of the heretics who hold specifically eternalist views, this body is a person. In the beginning, it is born, and during the first half of life, the faculties and aggregates develop and expand. This is *fullness* (*gang*). After the first half of life, the faculties diminish and cease during old age; this is *exhaustion* (*zag*). Thus birth and the aggregates join together in the space between one life and the next due to your karma, and this is *a person* (*gang zag*). This person is the self. The "I" is the eternal intellect. Just like a little bird flying away when its cage is smashed, after the aggregates cease, another set of aggregates are joined and grasped in the space between this life and the next. That which grasps them is the self. The nature of this self is like a completely clear crystal. It is obscured by darkness, dust, and sentient beings, and these three things give rise to *the intellect*. From the intellect, conceptualization arises. When things are labeled by the various concepts, that is saṃsāra. The method for reversing the causes of saṃsāra is nonconceptualization, which purifies the intellect. When the intellect is purified, then darkness, dust, and sentient beings are purified as well. Then you obtain the pure nature of mind, which is like a crystal. At this point, this is what is called *nirvāṇa*.

Then there are four types of noble hearer: (i) the hearers who fall, (ii) the hearers who convert, (iii) the hearers who emanate, and (iv) the hearers who pacify. The hearers who fall are fearful of the compounded things of the three realms and cultivate nirvāṇa with conviction. Once they have exhausted gross perceptions, they see the path of peace, and this is what they call nirvāṇa. In this situation, when a little bit of clairvoyance arises, they are able to see their own rebirth in a future state. Because they think that they have already attained nirvāṇa, when they see these further rebirths, they exclaim "even the Buddha's dharma is false!" Thus they fall into the state of a denizen of hell.

The hearers who convert initially enter the vehicle of the hearers, then later meet a spiritual guide who practices the greater vehicle, and they convert to the greater vehicle. The hearers who emanate are fully perfected buddhas like Subhuti and Śāriputra. In order to bring others to the greater vehicle, they display the forms of hearers as a skillful means. The hearers who pacify label all phenomena with the four general features: they understand all phenomena to be impermanent, suffering, empty, and without a self. They engage in the four noble truths: understand suffering, renounce its origin, actualize its cessation, and cultivate the path. Then, weary with saṃsāra, they put it behind them and have faith in nirvāṇa. They train themselves, pacify themselves, and apply themselves to nirvāṇa. Stopping the mental consciousness, they engage in the nonself of persons, but they do not engage in the nonself of phenomena. Although they clear away the obscurations of emotional afflictions, they do not clear away conceptual obscurations. Though they have a personal insight, they lack the means. Though they accomplish their own personal benefit, they don't consider the benefit of others. Because they grasp the essential meaning as a dissolution into peace and nothingness, they consider nirvāṇa to be a one-sided peacefulness.

The view of the noble solitary buddhas is this: by means of their personal insight and without relying on a spiritual guide, they understand how all phenomena arise through causes and conditions and are fearful of worldly phenomena. They consider that once they have stopped all suffering, the ultimate truth is pure, stainless, bright and luminous, and unknown to worldly intellects but known and engaged in by the intellects of noble ones. This expansive peace is the state of nirvāṇa. Having understood this for themselves, they cultivate it on their own. They do not teach the dharma verbally to sentient beings, but they do instruct via a variety of magical emanations.

As for the greater vehicle, there are two types: (i) Vijñānavāda and (ii) Madhyamaka. The view of the Vijñānavāda is as follows: All phenomena are nonexistent. They are merely seen by one's own deluded, conceptualizing intellect, but ultimately they are nonexistent. This is like a sick person who cannot apprehend anything, or like someone who has eaten the leaves of the nightshade, and sees hair-thin circles and needles when looking at the sky. That which is insubstantial appears real due to the power of delusion. They label everything according to three features: (i) the conceptualized, (ii) the dependent, and (iii) the accomplished. The phenomena that appear with the feature of conceptualization and the feature of dependence are not existent. Those with the feature of accomplishment are ultimately not nonexistent. When one is freed from the extremes of existence and nonexistence, and freed from subject and object, then wisdom appears immediately like a lamp's being blown out by the wind. Ultimately, wisdom is not nonexistent. If it were nonexistent, there would be no meaning to having the proper view and behavior.

The Madhyamaka is also twofold: (i) Yoga Madhyamaka and (ii) Sautrantika Madhyamaka. In Yoga Madhyamaka, the approach is similar to Vijñānavāda. Though ultimately the two Madhyamakas have a single meaning, they disagree regarding the view of the Vijñānavāda. The Sautrantika Madhyamaka say: "Is this immediate wisdom of yours claimed to be relative or ultimate? If you claim it is relative, then it can be true, but if you claim it is ultimate, it cannot be true." The reply is: "We claim that it is ultimate." And the response: "You say that immediate wisdom is free from the extremes of existence and nonexistence, and free from subject and object, and then you also say that ultimate truth is not nonexistent. So it cannot be free from subject and object, and it must have features that can be apprehended."

This is the view of Sautrantika Madhyamaka: All phenomena arise dependently. Both kinds of Madhyamaka agree on this. Because all phenomena arise dependently, in the relative truth they are magical illusions, like the moon in water or a mirage; they are not nonexistent. In the ultimate truth, the space of reality is nondual, free from the four extremes, without birth or cessation, transcending the realm of spoken or written language, without acceptance or rejection, not any kind of substance, not remaining or ceasing, free from subject and object, and without the merest atom of features or apprehension.

Having understood and clarified how everything is pure in this way, your engagement in the nonself of persons and phenomena is fully realized. You know—nondualistically and inseparably—the single taste of the space in which all phenomena are uncreated, the space of self and phenomena, the perfection of insight, and the way that everything is pure. With the insight that cultivates this, you sit with the mind in equanimity.

6

DEBATE

MOHEYAN AND THE DEBATE

Though the image of Zen in the later Tibetan tradition is inseparable from a historical narrative about a debate between the Chinese monk Moheyan and the Indian monk Kamalaśīla, there is no reason to view this narrative as a historically accurate documentary account; in fact, it would be highly unwise to do so. As discussed in the introduction, the earliest version of the Tibetan debate story comes from the *Testimony of Ba,* the earliest surviving copies of which were probably written in the twelfth century. The debate story here seems to be associated with a rivalry between two Tibetan clans. As its title suggests, this narrative puts members of the Ba clan at the forefront of developments in the establishment of Buddhism in Tibet. Clan rivalries were endemic in Tibetan society, and during the Tibetan imperial period, there are several examples of rivalry between the Ba and Dro clans.

In *Testimony of Ba,* members of the Ba clan play a large role in the defeat of Moheyan, who is said to have been supported by the queen from the Dro clan. And we know from other sources (see chapter 9), that members of the Dro clan were patrons of Zen teachers.[1] From the perspective of these clan rivalries, the debate story in the *Testimony of Ba* can be viewed as providing a precedent dating back to the time of the Tibetan empire for the rejection of Moheyan's lineage and those of the Dro clan who supported it. Subsequent versions of the debate story in later Tibetan histories change the emphasis so that it is Chinese Buddhism as a whole, represented as the embodiment of the instantaneous approach, that is rejected. In these later works, the function of the story was no longer to establish the superiority of a particular clan's claims to inherit the imperial Buddhist agenda but to give an imperial precedent for arguments that only Buddhist lineages that could be shown to come from India were authentic.

The earlier Chinese version of the debate story is quite different, which is not surprising, as its context and function differ from those of the *Testimony of Ba* and later Tibetan histories. The full title of the Chinese text is in the *Ratification of the True Principle of Instantaneous Awakening in the Greater Vehicle*. It comprises several groups of questions and answers collected together by a Chinese official called Wangxi, who was once assistant to the Hexi Inspectorate, the local government body whose remit would have included Dunhuang. Attached to these questions and answers, Wangxi wrote a preface in which he explained how they came to be written down. The preface tells of the Tibetan emperor's bringing Buddhism to Tibet by inviting to Lhasa teachers from India and China, including Moheyan. At the Tibetan court, Moheyan gave initiations into Zen practice and had some success in converting members of the Tibetan nobility. However, he also attracted the ire of the Indian teachers, who attempted to have him banned from teaching:

> It was first in the year Chen (792) that our grand master was informed of an edict, which read: "The Indian monk and others have declared, in a memorial, that the system of Zen called "Sudden Awakening" taught by the Chinese monk does not correspond at all with what was preached by the Buddha, and they demand that it is stopped immediately." Our master of Zen began to laugh softly and said: "Nonsense! Are the beings of this country so lacking in the suitability for the greater vehicle that they let themselves be molested by the armies of the Evil One? Do they wish their own destruction, taking the dharma that I teach as contrary to the principles of the Buddha?" ... And he memorialized in these terms: "I humbly ask His Divine Majesty to demand from the Indian monk his objections, so that we may discuss together and check the meaning of the sacred texts. I know what to expect; and if my doctrine seems the least aberrant,

then I ask that it be terminated!" The king agreed, and the Indian monk and his group, for all the months of a year, reviewed the sūtras to seek their meaning and presented more and more questions, trying to find fault with our master. But he whose mind clarifies the truth to the depths of this net gave an answer to each question, just like the purifying wind rolling away the clouds and opening the eyes of the distant sky, or the precious mirror in which, as soon as day approaches, all images appear distinctly.[2]

This then is the context for the questions and answers that follow. But the story does not end here. According to Wangxi, it was not Moheyan's answers alone that swung the issue, but a protest from his Tibetan students. Two monks set fire to their hair and cut themselves with knives in protest. Another thirty threatened to renounce their robes if the Tibetan king ruled against Moheyan. Given that this was in the early stages of the establishment of a Tibetan monastic community, such a threat might well have been taken seriously. According to Wangxi, it completely destroyed the morale of the opposing side, who gave up the debate. Some elements of this story appear virtually unchanged in the Tibetan version, including the self-harming monks. But there are also clear differences.

For one thing, in Wangxi's account, this is not a debate but an extended discussion taking place over the course of a year. The location of the protagonists is not given, and it is not stated that Moheyan and the Indian monk actually met face to face during the course of the year; questions and answers might equally have been written down and passed back and forth. The dramatic and highly charged symbolism of a single debate at the great monastery of Samye, presided over by the Tibetan emperor himself, looks like a later elaboration of the story. The other significant difference between the two accounts is the emperor's final verdict, which according to Wangxi, was entirely positive toward Moheyan and his teachings:

On the fifteenth day of the first month of the year Sui (794), a great edict was at last announced: "The Zen doctrine taught by Moheyan is a perfect development founded in the texts of the sūtras. It has not the slightest error. Henceforth, the religious and lay are authorized to practice and exercise under this teaching!"[3]

Conversely, in the *Testimony of Ba,* the emperor rules that the instantaneous approach is invalid and that monks must follow Nāgārjuna, an ironic statement in itself considering the importance of Nāgārjuna and his teachings in the Tibetan Zen manuscripts. Wangxi was himself a student of Moheyan, so his account does have the primacy of being much the earliest, but he is by no means an impartial observer. His account is, like the *Testimony,* a narrative designed to have a particular effect. Debate narratives have played an important role in Chinese Buddhism in shaping the way traditions developed. In Moheyan's time, for example, there was a popular account of a debate convened by Shenhui at the monastery of Huatai in which he successfully defended his radical version of Zen. Despite the wide circulation of this account, John Jørgensen suspects that it comprises "invented dialogues" and was actually written to cover up Shenhui's failure in the debate.[4] Thus we have to regretfully conclude that the *Ratification* offers little more historical certainty than the *Testimony.* It's narratives all the way down.[5]

There is one other early account, though it is very brief. In the late ninth or early tenth century, the Tibetan scholar Nub Sangye Yeshe mentions both Moheyan and Kamalaśīla in his *Lamp for the Eyes of Contemplation* in a brief account of the transmission of Buddhism to Tibet, but he does not appear to be aware of any conflict between them. The passage seems to suggest that doubts that arose among the Tibetan emperor and the monks subsequent to the visit of Moheyan were addressed by Kamalaśīla, among others. This may be a reference to the compositions by Kamalaśīla known as *The Stages of Meditation.* These works and the *Ratification* do deal with similar issues, though from quite different perspectives and without either text showing any awareness of the other. It looks like both were written for the benefit of the Tibetan court, each defending a particular approach to teaching Buddhism, but neither gives any reason to believe that the authors met or even corresponded.[6]

In any case, as we saw in the introduction, Zen continued to be transmitted and practiced in Tibet over the centuries that followed the activities of Moheyan and Kamalaśīla, at least as late as the thirteenth century. Later Tibetan histories, such as the influential fourteenth-century history of Buddhism by Butön added further elements to the story that served to demonize Moheyan and, by association, Chinese Buddhism.

For example, Moheyan is said to have gone back to China and sent from there Chinese assassins who killed Kamalaśīla. Such fantastic tales further served to make the point that Tibet, not China, was the true inheritor of authentic Indian Buddhism.

THE ROLE OF THE *RATIFICATION*

When the *Ratification* was published by Paul Demiéville in 1952, his translation of the text was accompanied by erudite and lengthy footnotes bringing in many other texts relevant to the period. It was one of the most successful attempts to pin the free-floating world of traditional Zen narratives to known historical figures, such as the Tibetan emperor Tri Song Detsen, who ruled in the second half of the eighth century.[7] However, we should not lose sight of the fact that the manuscript copies of the *Ratification* were written much later, in the tenth century. One thing we can be sure of is that whoever wrote the surviving copies of the *Ratification* and the *Testimony of Ba* did not do so to provide an accurate account of events in the eighth century for scholars in the twentieth and twenty-first. Modern historians' use of the manuscripts differs so radically from their earlier functions that it may be difficult to leave the former in the background in order to reconstruct the latter. But this is necessary if we are not to treat these texts naively as documentary sources for the events they describe.

The most complete version of the *Ratification* is found in Pelliot chinois 4646, which is in the loose-leaf pothi format that derives from Indian palm leaf books. It was the most popular form for Tibetan Buddhist manuscripts at Dunhuang but was relatively rare among the Chinese manuscripts. Like many manuscripts, this is a compendium, containing five texts:

Vimalakīrti-nirdeśa-sūtra
Saptaśatika-prajñāpāramitā-sūtra
*Ratification of the True Principle of Instantaneous Awakening
    in the Greater Vehicle*
Treatise on Observing the Mind, by Shenxiu
Sutra of the Method of Meditation

Clearly, if the *Ratification* was considered to be a text of primarily historical interest, it is in strange company here. The manuscript begins with two sūtras that were popular among Zen lineages and are often quoted in Zen texts. The questions and answers of the *Ratification* fall in the middle of the manuscript and are followed by two texts on the methods of meditation. The arrangement of texts is reminiscent of Pelliot tibétain 116. Scriptural texts are followed by a series of questions and answers that works toward finding a place for the Zen methods within the accepted Buddhist structures, with two discussions of the practice of meditation coming toward the end. Thus this manuscript might be another collection of source material for sermons or initiation ceremonies.

Then there is the Tibetan version of the *Ratification*. The Tibetan manuscript, comprising IOL Tib J 703 and Pelliot tibétain 823, is not complete but contains at least two texts—the Tibetan *Ratification* and another question and answer text, the *Single Method of Nonapprehension*, which appears in Pelliot tibétain 116 and has already been discussed in chapter 1. The *Single Method* is in fact very similar to the *Ratification* in its sequence of questions and answers that allow for the gradual building of a doctrinal position. In fact, the questions in the *Single Method* give much more of an impression of actual objections than those in the Tibetan *Ratification*; for example, "Some say that those who cultivate only the accumulation of wisdom cannot attain full and perfect buddhahood, and this is because they do not practice the accumulation of merit." Nevertheless, there is no suggestion in the *Single Method* that this is a record of an actual debate; rather the objections are the framework within which a position harmonizing the instantaneous and gradual approaches is worked though.

Many other Chinese and Tibetan Zen treatises use the question and answer format as well, and the tone of the questions in these varies from polite requests for clarification to the oppositional querying of apparent contradictions and errors. In brief, these are the conventions of a genre.[8] We know that the ritualized enactment of these questions and answers in a debate was itself a practice in Zen lineages. An account by the Japanese monk Ennin (793–864) shows how formalized debate worked within the standard teaching ritual:

After that, the weina (K. *ina*) came in front of the high seat and read out the reasons for holding the meeting and the separate names of the patrons and the things they had donated, after which he passed this document to the lecturer, who, grasping his chowry, read the patrons' names one by one and made supplications for each individually. After that the debaters argued the principles, raising questions. While they were raising a question, the lecturer would hold up his chowry, and when a questioner had finished asking his question, he would lower it and then raise it again, thank [the questioner] for his question, and then answer it. They recorded both the questions and the answers. It was the same as in Japan, except that the rite of [pointing out doctrinal] difficulties was somewhat different. After lowering his hand at his side three times and before making any explanation, [a debater] would suddenly proclaim the difficulty, shouting with all his might like a man enraged, and the lecturer would accept the problem and would reply without raising problems in return.[9]

This account maps closely to the more adversarial questions and answers in the *Ratification:* the difficulty is raised and then answered "without raising any problems in return." The element of playacting in the ritual practice described here by Ennin shows how the drama of the debate scenario was incorporated into what was in fact an ordinary nonadversarial ritual setting. And this helps us to see how even Wangxi's preface to the *Ratification,* setting the scene of the questions and answers in a dramatic historical narrative, could have worked in the scene setting for ritualized debates like these.

THE TIBETAN MANUSCRIPTS

The fact that the questions and answers in Pelliot tibétain 823 matched up with some of those in the *Ratification* was first shown by Yoshiro Imaeda (1975). Imaeda showed that most of the questions in the Tibetan manuscript matched up with those in the *Ratification* that were introduced as "old questions," which come at the beginning of the text. This suggested that the Tibetan manuscript represented an earlier text that was incorporated into the *Ratification* when it was compiled. If these questions and answers did emerge from the activities of Moheyan at the Tibetan court, it could be that the Tibetan versions were the originals, later translated into Chinese; equally, they could have been composed in Chinese and translated into Tibetan for the benefit of the Tibetan court. In any case, this strongly suggests that the *Ratification* is a hybrid drawn from various sources, one of which is the Tibetan text in Pelliot tibétain 823.

The manuscript Pelliot tibétain 823 is a concertina, missing both its beginning and end. The translation below unites Pelliot tibétain 823 with another part of the same original manuscript, which had become separated at some point, so that the two parts ended up in Paris and London, respectively. The London manuscript IOL Tib J 703 adds another two folios to the end, which instead of further questions and answers gives a long scriptural quotation on the importance of practicing meditation rather than just studying the dharma. The very end of the manuscript is still missing, but this scriptural coda may have been the conclusion to the Tibetan *Ratification*.

The beginning of Pelliot tibétain 823 is still missing, but the beginning of the text of the Tibetan *Ratification* appears elsewhere in another manuscript. This is Pelliot tibétain 827, roughly scribbled lines written on the back of a single panel from a Chinese scroll. These lines contain two texts, neither of which has been given a title. The first is very similar to some other works by Moheyan on five methods of meditation; here the five methods are different (and successively better) ways of dealing with experience:

1. Not experiencing perceptual activity
2. Chasing experience
3. Not allowing the perception of experience to arise
4. Peacefulness through experiencing the arising of perception
5. Not chasing experience

This is clearly a text about meditation, with similarities to the work by Shenxiu that was written after the *Ratification* on the manuscript Pelliot chinois 4646. The text that follows it is the one that overlaps with Pelliot tibétain 823, providing us with the lost opening lines of the Tibetan *Ratification*. These questions and answers match up with the Chinese *Ratification*, with one exception: the first question and answer in the Chinese *Ratification* is, in the Tibetan text, just an introductory paragraph (that is, the answer is here, but not the question).[10] This works well in the Tibetan text, as this introductory paragraph sets up the assertions that are queried and unpacked in the questions and answers that follow:

> In the scriptures of the greater vehicle, it says that anybody who is free from all discrimination is a buddha. Observe the mind and purify discrimination and habitual imprints. This is what is taught and described in the sūtras of the greater vehicle.

The first six of the questions and answers that follow explicate this pithy statement. The specific scriptures that are being invoked here are named; the *Laṅkāvatāra* appears repeatedly alongside the Perfection of Wisdom sūtras. The nature of discrimination (Tib. *'du shes,* Ch. *wangxiang,* Skt. *saṃjñā*) is described as perception that is contaminated with conceptual activity, "grasping at objects and features." The habitual imprints (Tib. *bag chags,* Ch. *xiqi,* Skt. *vedanā*) are not explained, which suggests that the audience for the text would be expected to understand this level of Buddhist doctrine. In questions five and six, the crucial practice of observing the mind (Tib. *sems la blta ba,* Ch. *kanxin*) is described (for more on this, see chapter 7).

Further questions and answers address related topics, particularly the relevance of the six perfections. The tenth question and answer, which asks for justification in the scriptures and provides it with quotations, is much longer than the others and may be a later addition. That the Tibetan *Ratification,* which seems to represent the earliest stratum of the Chinese *Ratification,* may itself be the result of textual development over time is also suggested by the existence of another text. *The Principle of Nonconceptualization* (found in Pelliot tibétain 21) comprises the third, fourth, and seventh answers from the *Ratification,* without the questions. We can't know whether this brief text came before or after the *Ratification,* but it shows the fluid and changeable nature of these texts.

Certainly the Chinese *Ratification,* with its internal distinction between old and new questions, is a composite product. What might this mean? It could be that we should take Wangxi's preface at face value, in which case the composite nature of the text is due to the exchanges of questions and answers between Moheyan and the Indian monks over the course of a year. It could also mean that the text is not quite as it is described in the preface. Instead, it might be a compendium of various question and answer texts with some association to Moheyan, pulled together and put in the context of the Tibetan debate as a narrative framework. In any case, if we look at the texts that were copied alongside the *Ratification* in the Chinese and Tibetan manuscripts, we get a better idea of its original function, which is likely to have been very different from the uses that it has been put to by historians.

TRANSLATION

In the scriptures of the greater vehicle, it is said that anybody who is free from all discrimination is a buddha.[11] Observe the mind and purify discrimination and habitual imprints. This is what is taught and described in the sūtras of the greater vehicle.[12]

QUESTION: Which scriptures do you mean when you say "the greater vehicle"?

The *Laṅkāvatāra sūtra* says that the greater and lesser vehicles are seen due to the existence of false discrimination and that if one is free from false discrimination, one does not speak of the greater and lesser vehicles; indeed, one does not even use the word "vehicle." This is the context of the term "greater vehicle."

QUESTION: Where is it said that anybody who is free from discrimination is called a buddha?

It is taught in the *Vajracchedikā,* the *Mahāprajñāpāramitā,* the *Gandhavyūha,* the *Laṅkāvatāra,* and all other sūtras.

QUESTION: You talk about "all discrimination." What is this discrimination?

"Discrimination" is the mind's movement and constant grasping at objects and features. "All" refers to the fact that it arises in all minds, from those of hell beings to those of buddhas. Again, the *Laṅkāvatāra sūtra* says that all phenomena are without intrinsic nature, yet they are all seen by false discrimination.[13]

QUESTION: What is wrong with discrimination?[14]

All sentient beings are in full possession of omniscient wisdom. They are corrupted by emotional obscurations and all the things that cause long-term cycling in saṃsāra and the three lower realms. The *Vajracchedikā* also says to abandon discrimination.

QUESTION: How does one "observe the mind"?

Turn away from the six sense doors and then observe the mind. If discrimination stirs, do not think that it exists or does not exist, is pure or impure, is empty or not empty, and so on. Be without concepts, not even thinking of not thinking. It is said in the *Vimalakīrti* too that not conceptualizing is enlightenment.

QUESTION: What is the method for purifying discrimination and habitual imprints?

When false discrimination stirs, experience it. If this experience of birth and death is not learned or practiced in the style of discrimination and there is no attachment to it, then each thought will be immediately liberated. The *Vajracchedikā* and the great *Mahāratnakūṭa* also say that when you do not acquire even the slightest bit of dharma, this is the supreme enlightenment.

QUESTION: Are other religious approaches such as the six perfections necessary?

In conventional truth there are six perfections, while in the ultimate teachings they are said to be just methods. Yet that does not mean that they are unnecessary. The scriptures that speak of the ultimate truth beyond ordinary thinking do not even discuss whether other dharma methods such as the six perfections are necessary or not. This is explained extensively in the sūtras.

QUESTION: If the six perfections are necessary, how is one to practice these methods?

When you are practicing the six perfections and the like, there is an outer and an inner way. In the inner way, you liberate yourself. In the outer way, you bring benefit to others. As for the method that you practice, sūtras such as the *Laṅkāvatāra* and *Sutra of Altruism* say that when you practice, you should not conceptualize or think about any phenomena, you should be free of the three spheres (of agent, action, and object) so that they are like illusions, and you should practice without even trying to achieve not thinking about anything.

QUESTION: When practicing this religious approach, how much does one need to do to attain liberation?

The *Laṅkāvatāra* and *Vajracchedikā* say that when you are free from all discrimination, you are a buddha. When those with sharp faculties cultivate this, they are free from all false discrimination and habitual imprints and are immediately liberated.

QUESTION: What is the merit in practicing these dharma scriptures?

The merit of not conceptualizing and not thinking cannot be measured by analytical thought; you should instead look to buddha thought. Let me explain just a fragment of this: it is said in the *Prajñāpāramitā* that for all sentient beings—from the stages of gods and humans, to hearers and solitary realizers, all the way to those who are established in supreme enlightenment—the merit of studying the scriptures of the perfection of wisdom and having confidence in them is vast beyond counting or calculation. Why is that? Because everyone, gods and humans, hearers and solitary realizers, and the supremely enlightened, arise from the perfection of wisdom. Yet for those who talk of calculations, the perfection of wisdom will not arise. What then is the perfection of wisdom? It is taught that the perfection of wisdom is without features, without acceptance or rejection, and without attachment. Also, from the *Tathāgataguṇācitya*:

> If someone were to spend an uncountable eon making as many propitiations and offerings to the tathāgatas as there are particles in the three-thousandfold universe, or if those buddhas who have not yet reached nirvāṇa were to fill the three-thousandfold universe with stūpas ornamented with the seven types of precious stones and propitiate them for an uncountable eon, still the merit of being free from all doubts in this inconceivable dharma scripture is a hundred thousand times, no, countless times greater.

And from the *Vajracchedikā*:

> If someone were to fill the three-thousandfold universe with the seven types of precious stones and make an offering of it, or give up as many bodies as there are sands in the River Ganges, the merit of hearing a single four-line stanza would still be incomparably and immeasurably greater.

This is explained extensively in these and all other sūtras. They also say that there is no other merit apart from buddhahood.

QUESTION: Once discrimination has been abandoned and there is no thought or conceptualization, how does omniscient wisdom arise?

You possess the pure nature from the beginning, so wisdom arises spontaneously when there is no stirring of false thought and you have abandoned discrimination. The *Gandhavyūha* and *Laṅkāvatāra* say that this is like the sun's coming out from behind the clouds, the clearing of muddy water, the cleansing of a mirror, or the extraction of silver from ore.

QUESTION: How is the benefit of beings achieved by nonconceptual wisdom?

The benefit of beings is achieved without intention or analysis. This is explained extensively in the *Tathāgataguṇācitya*, which teaches that this is like the way the sun and moon shine on everything, a wish-fulfilling jewel produces anything, and the great earth gives rise to everything.

QUESTION: If there are three kinds of grasping—grasping at objects, grasping at consciousness, and grasping at what lies between—which scriptures teach this?

This is spoken of in the greater vehicle scriptures of the inconceivable *Prajñāpāramitā,* and equally, that which cannot be grasped is taught extensively in the *Prajñāpāramitā.*

QUESTION: If this is in these scriptures, it should be elaborated upon in other sūtras, so where else is it taught?

All of the teachings from the sūtras explain only the false discrimination of sentient beings. If one is free from discrimination, then there is no dharma to be taught. Thus the *Laṅkāvatāra* says that all sūtras talk about the discrimination of sentient beings, but the pure truth is not found in words.

QUESTION: How do buddhas explain the discrimination of sentient beings?[15]

The buddhas' omniscient wisdom and their range of activity is inconceivable and cannot be known through measurement. They cannot be grasped by the conjectures of any ordinary consciousness, nor can they be understood through insight. Thus, there is no point in conjecturing "they intend this" or "they do that." As it says in the sūtras, since one who is free from all discrimination is a buddha, you should view the mind and purify all discrimination and habitual imprints.[16]

Anyone who asks about this
Should listen to me, one of the buddha's sons.

This teaching of perfect buddhahood
Is not accomplished merely by studying it.

Like a person of little strength
Being swept away into the sea
And dying of thirst:
Such is the dharma without cultivation.

Like one who gives away food and drink
To a multitude of living beings
Then starves to death himself:
Such is the dharma without cultivation.

Like a doctor
With every medicine in his possession
Dying of a stomach complaint:
Such is the dharma without cultivation.[17]

Like a person born near a royal palace
In which every happiness can be found
Yet having neither food nor clothes:
Such is the dharma without cultivation.

Like a deaf person who is a fine singer
And player of musical instruments
Bringing delight only to others:
Such is the dharma without cultivation.

Like a blind painter
Who paints in the middle of the marketplace
But cannot see anything himself:
Such is the dharma without cultivation.

Like a boatman on a great ocean
Who saves many creatures

But stays on himself and dies:
Such is the dharma without cultivation.

Like someone who tells all
About the wonders to be found on the road
But fails to obtain any himself:
Such is the dharma without cultivation.[18]

7

OBSERVING THE MIND

THE ZEN MASTER MOHEYAN

Though we know that the monk known as Moheyan was a major influence on Tibetan Zen, we know little about his background. The
preface to the *Ratification* includes among Moheyan's teachers a certain
Xiangmo Zang, who was one of the objects of Shenhui's polemics against
the Northern School. For this reason, Moheyan has often been identified
as a representative of the Northern School, but this is problematic. First,
the name "Northern School" (*Beizong*) was not a self-identification but
a polemical label used by Shenhui and his followers—who identified
themselves as the "Southern School"—to refer to other more successful Zen lineages. The Zen teachers criticized by Shenhui identified their
lineages with other names, such as the "East Mountain Dharma Gate"
(*Dongshan famen*), or as the lineage of the *Laṅkāvatāra*.[1]

Second, Moheyan may have actually counted Shenhui among his own
teachers. The *Chan Letter* of Zongmi (780–841) lists Moheyan as one
of the students of Shenhui. Since Moheyan was a generation younger
than Shenhui, this is quite possible chronologically, and differences in
doctrine are not enough to rule out the possibility, considering the fluid
nature of the doctrinal distinctions in the Chinese Dunhuang Zen manuscripts, not to mention the Tibetan ones.[2]

This doctrinal fluidity is characteristic of the manuscripts. As we
have seen in chapter 2, the compendiums of masters' teachings in Pelliot
tibétain 116 and other manuscripts include Shenhui alongside teachers associated with the Northern School. Moheyan himself taught the

tathāgata meditation that is said to have been a specialty of Shenhui (see chapter 3) and used the phrase "observing the mind," previously associated with Shenxiu. Thus to deny the possibility that Moheyan could have studied with Shenhui as well as with a teacher associated with the Northern School would be to apply rigid distinctions between schools to a time when these did not exist.

Certainly Shenhui was polemical in his attacks on other teachers; this does not mean that none of those who were instructed by him ever went to other famous teachers. Other students of Shenhui, rather than slavishly following his oppositional approach, attempted to make his teachings more applicable to practice by bringing them into dialogue with established norms.[3] The texts of Moheyan translated here show a similar concern with harmonizing the doctrine of single method and instantaneous result with the existence of various practices and the need for a graduated approach.

The image of Moheyan changed again in Tibet many centuries after his death. In the early tenth-century *Lamp for the Eyes of Contemplation,* Moheyan is said to be the seventh in the lineage of masters beginning with Bodhidharma. Much later, in the fourteenth century, *The Minister's Edict* reworked this passage from *Lamp for the Eyes of Contemplation* to present Moheyan as an expert in the tantras:

> Heshang Moheyan practiced the twelve methods. In the secret mantra of the greater vehicle, he received the many stages of initiation and displayed many maṇḍalas.[4]

Though some have seen this as a deliberate distortion, it is supported in a surprising place—the Chinese text of the *Ratification,* in which Wangxi tells us that when Moheyan arrived in Lhasa, "our grand master conferred a secret Zen initiation and demonstrated brilliantly his magisterial authority."[5] What form might this secret initiation have taken? We have already discussed in the introduction the role that the ritual of bestowing bodhisattva precepts on an ordination platform played in propagating Chinese Zen practices during the eighth century. There is little doubt that tantric Buddhist concepts became associated with these ordination platform rituals. For example, Yixing (683–727), a student of the tantric teacher Śubhākarasiṃha, established a platform called Five Buddhas' Perfect Awareness Platform, an explicit reference to tantric maṇḍalas. And from Dunhuang itself, we have a popular text explaining in detail the rituals associated with ordination platforms, drawing on esoteric Buddhist practices while remaining firmly in a Zen lineage.[6]

Given the competition for royal patronage between Moheyan and the Indian masters that we see in the *Ratification,* it is possible that Moheyan would have employed the language and perhaps some of the rituals of esoteric Buddhism when presenting himself to the Tibetan court. In Tibet, as in China, teachers of esoteric Buddhist methods would have been able to present a range of practices drawn from the sūtras and tantras, creating some pressure for Chinese teachers to match this in some way. It is thus interesting that the longer text translated below ends with two quotations from scripture, which are given without attribution to specific texts. One of them is not from a sūtra, but from the *Guhyasamāja tantra,* one of the central scriptures of mahāyoga.

Though *The Minister's Edict* presented a positive picture of Moheyan in accordance with the ideal of a tantric master that was dominant in fourteenth-century Tibet, this was actually the point at which the last Tibetan Zen lineages were dying. The general trend was in the direction of demonizing Moheyan as a proponent of a misguided meditation practice: the suppression of mental activity to produce a state of blank unawareness. That this is a historically misleading version of Moheyan's teaching is clear from the texts translated below; yet it was clearly a useful trope in the practice of instructing students in meditation. It also helped maintain an ideology in which Tibet represented the only complete and correct transmission of the Buddha's word.[7] Nevertheless, even the simplified depiction of Moheyan's position in the *Testimony* contained enough to convince some Tibetans that he was being misrepresented. For example, the eighteenth-century treasure revealer Jigme Lingpa wrote:

> If nonrecollection and nonmentation entail the offense of rejecting the wisdom of differentiating analysis, then the Perfection of Wisdom sūtras of the Conqueror also entail this fault. Therefore, what the view of the Heshang actually was can be known by a perfect buddha, and no one else.[8]

MOHEYAN'S MEDITATION PRACTICE

The access provided by the Dunhuang manuscripts to Moheyan's own work shows exactly how the debate narrative in the *Testimony* distorted his position. The words put into Moheyan's mouth in the earliest known version are as follows:

> By the power of virtuous and nonvirtuous acts generated by the mind's conceptualization, sentient beings cycle round in saṃsāra experiencing their karmic results in the higher and lower realms. Whoever neither thinks anything nor does anything, will be liberated from saṃsāra. This being the case, do not think anything at all! As for teachings on the ten aspects of religious practice, such as generosity, they are to be taught solely to those lacking karmic virtue: those of the lower classes, and those with dull faculties and weak intellects.[9]

This passage makes Moheyan an advocate of an antipractice doctrine. In fact, rather than deprecating practice, in his own works, Moheyan provides relatively detailed instructions on meditation. In the treatise translated here, Moheyan describes the practice known as "observing the mind" (Tib. *sems la bltas,* Ch. *kanxin*) thus:

> When they engage in meditation, they should view their own mind. Since nothing exists there, they have no thoughts. If conceptual thoughts move, they should experience them. "How should we experience them?" Whatever thoughts arise should not be designated as moving or not moving. They should not be designated as existing or not existing. They should not be designated as virtuous or nonvirtuous. They should not be designated as afflicted or pure. They should not be designated as any kind of phenomenon at all. If the movement of mind is experienced in this way, it has no nature. This is called "practicing the dharma path."

Here Moheyan complements the repeated negations in his meditation instructions with positive language about the illuminating function of the mind. Rather than suppressing the mind's movement, he advocates instead a form of experience without analysis. The Tibetan word that I have translated as "experience" is *tshor,* which is itself a translation for the Chinese *jue.* In translations of Buddhist Sanskrit, both words can stand for the Sanskrit *vedanā,* "feeling" or "sensation," which is one of the twelve links of dependent arising and therefore fundamentally part of the process of saṃsāra. In Zen literature, on the other hand, the meaning of *jue* is more positive, a connation that may be drawn from earlier Chinese literature such as the *Zhuangzi,* in which *jue* refers to a clear and correct form of awareness.

For Moheyan, *tshor* is a key concept for explaining meditation. It is a basic state of awareness that is neither positive nor negative in itself. As the *Summary,* the second text translated below, shows, it is not the presence of experience that makes the difference between inferior and superior stages of meditation, but what is done or not done with that experience. The mental state of blankness that Moheyan and, by extension, Chinese Buddhism in general is supposed to have endorsed is actually specifically criticized in this text. Here, the suppression of mental movement and the state of resting in peace are the third and fourth of the methods, inferior and incorrect in comparison to the fifth, in which "each thought is liberated as soon as it comes." A concluding line to this text shows the level of distortion in the later Tibetan view that Moheyan promoted the suppression of thoughts:

> Thus do not suppress discrimination. Do not correct anything that arises, like throwing away something unpleasant. Letting it subside on its own, do not chase after it.[10]

This then is what Moheyan calls "observing the mind." The same phrase is used in the description of meditation practice in the *Ratification,* also attributed to Moheyan:

> Turn away from the six sense gates and then view the mind. If discrimination stirs, do not think that it exists or does not exist, is pure or impure, is empty or not empty, and so on. Be without concepts, not even thinking of not thinking. . . . When false

discrimination stirs, experience it. If this experience of birth and death is not learned or practiced in the style of discrimination, and there is no attachment to it, then each thought will be immediately liberated.

The description here is terse but suggests a technique of introversion, turning attention away from the sensory impressions of the six gates (sight, hearing, touch, smell, taste and *manas* or mental consciousness) and toward a "mind" that remains in the absence of the senses. In the Chinese version of the *Ratification,* this practice of turning away is introduced in a quote from the *Mahā-uṣṇīṣa sūtra,* which states that once a single sense faculty is returned to its source, all six are liberated.[11] After this turning inward, the actual practice of observing the mind as described in the two passages above is a process of experiencing mental activity without becoming involved in judging or analyzing.

Meditation practice going under the name "observing the mind" was not specific to Moheyan; it is also to be seen in works attributed to earlier Zen masters, including Wolun (d. 626) and Shenxiu (607–706). A text by Wolun dedicated to the subject entitled *Meditation Master Wolun's Teaching on Observing the Mind* is found in the Chinese Dunhuang manuscripts. The practice of observing the mind is also invoked in several sūtras, including the *Mahā-uṣṇīṣa sūtra.*[12] If Moheyan's version of observing the mind differs from those of earlier masters such as Shenxiu, it is to simplify and exclude the more analytical aspects of viewing inherited from those earlier practices. Thus Moheyan's approach reconciles, or attempts to reconcile, the practices taught by Shenxiu and his students (including Moheyan's own teacher Xiangmo Zang) with the simple and instantaneous realization of the mind's true nature that Shenhui insisted upon.

This is, no doubt, a difficult task to accomplish. In his study of the texts translated here, Luis Gómez believes that Moheyan fails to present a coherent argument regarding whether methods such as the six perfections are necessary or not. Yet the three texts here, along with the one translated in chapter 2, present a consistent position on this question. According to Moheyan, the Buddhist practices exemplified by the six perfections are necessary for those who do not have the capability to see the nature of mind immediately. For those who can, the six perfections are not abandoned, but arise naturally out of the state of meditation. Thus his denial in the Chinese *Ratification* that such methods are necessary for those with sharp faculties is not "a fatal slip" as Gómez believes but is consistent with his position throughout the writings attributed to him.[13] Also, it is worth mentioning that this distinction between students of different capabilities was not an innovation of Moheyan's and continued to be used by Buddhist teachers from India and Tibet over the following centuries.[14]

THE MOHEYAN MANUSCRIPTS AND THEIR INTERRELATIONSHIPS

In all there are five Tibetan texts attributed to Moheyan found among the Dunhuang manuscripts, some of them in several different copies. This confirms the significance of Moheyan in the Tibetan transmission of Zen, as stated in the preface to the Chinese *Ratification*. The texts are as follows:

THE RATIFICATION OF THE TRUE PRINCIPLE

In its Tibetan version, this text is found in the incomplete manuscript comprising Pelliot tibétain 823 and IOL Tib J 703. This version is missing its beginning and end. Another copy, with the beginning of the text, is found in Pelliot tibétain 827. A different version, containing only some of the answers and none of the questions, is found in Pelliot tibétain 21. None of these manuscript copies contains an explicit attribution to Moheyan, so it is only by analogy to the Chinese version that we attribute them to him. Translated above in chapter 6.

MASTER MOHEYAN'S INTRODUCTION TO INSTANTANEOUS MEDITATION

This is the longest Tibetan text actually attributed to Moheyan. It begins on the two folios IOL Tib J 468 and continues through to IOL Tib J 709, part of the same original manuscript. There is a single folio missing between the two manuscripts (folio 3), and IOL Tib J 709 is also missing folios 5 and 6, so there are two major lacunae in the text. Since we have no other copies of the text, the continuity of the text across the lost folios is not certain, though there is a quote from the *Lamp for the Eyes of Contemplation* that shows that the text did continue across the first lacuna.[15] I am assuming here that the text also continued across the large gap of the missing fifth and sixth folios; there is no external evidence for this, but the final part of the text is thematically close to the other texts attributed to Moheyan, especially in the discussion of the six perfections. Translated below.

SUMMARY OF MASTER MOHEYAN'S INTRODUCTION TO INSTANTANEOUS MEDITATION

This text is much shorter than the one above, justifying the claim of its title to be a brief summary or condensed version of the longer text. To judge from the many versions that have survived in the manuscripts, it seems to have been popular. It is found in Pelliot tibétain 117, 812, and 813, and a slightly different text in Pelliot tibétain 827. It was also well known enough to be quoted by Nub Sangye Yeshe in *Lamp for the Eyes of Contemplation,* which includes a concluding line not found in the manuscripts. Translated below.

A BRIEF TEACHING ON HOW THE SIX OR TEN PERFECTIONS ARE INCLUDED IN NONCONCEPTUAL MEDITATION

This short text is dedicated to a theme that is also discussed in the *Ratification* and the *Introduction:* the relationship between the six perfections and the instantaneous style of meditation practice. The only complete version of the text is in Pelliot tibétain 116. Another version that is missing the end of the text is in Pelliot tibétain 117. Translation in chapter 2.

From the Teachings of Master Moheyan

This is merely a single line appearing in the *Single Method:* "Sit without thinking or conceptualizing in the space of reality free from thought." Note that this simple meditation instruction does not do justice to the more subtle explanations of meditation practice in other texts attributed to Moheyan. The various manuscript copies of the *Single Method* are discussed in chapter 1.

Luis Gómez also lists a brief text on the meaning of the Madhyamaka in Pelliot tibétain 812 that is attributed to Moheyan; however, this attribution is a mistaken correction of another name, meant to represent Haklenayaśas. A scribe who should have written "'Gal na yas" wrote "'Gal ya na," which was then "corrected" by somebody else to "Ma ha yan." A better copy of that text, with the name written properly, can be found in IOL Tib J 709.

All of these Moheyan texts were copied into manuscript compendiums along with other texts. There is no single manuscript gathering together all of Moheyan's texts. Thus we can say that Moheyan was an important figure for Tibetan Zen, but his works were treated in much the same way as the other similar Zen texts found in these manuscript compendiums.

The manuscripts containing the *Introduction* form a single compendium in loose-leaf pothi format (IOL Tib J 468 plus IOL Tib J 709 plus IOL Tib J 667). Unlike the other large compendium, Pelliot tibétain 116, this manuscript does not seem to have been arranged for a specific ritual purpose. All of the texts concern meditation and related practices. Since the manuscript is carefully written, probably by an educated monk or scribe, it does not appear to be the informal notes of a student. Judging from the style and contents, it may have been used as a source book for teaching or sermons. This compilation shows a deliberate interest in ratifying the Tibetan version of Zen, beginning as it does with a text by Moheyan, and ending with a text said to have been officially approved by Tri Song Detsen, the emperor during whose reign Moheyan is supposed to have visited Tibet. An interesting aspect of this manuscript's biography is seen on the verso of the final folio, which has been used for writing practice by a scribe who has written various text titles across it. The handwriting of this scribe matches that in the first and last panels of Pelliot tibétain 116. So this manuscript seems to have been owned, at a later stage, by the same person who collected and repaired the only other comparably large compendium of Zen texts.

Finally, Moheyan's *Summary* is copied into four different manuscript compendiums, always along with other texts relevant to Zen meditation practice. In the pothi manuscript Pelliot tibétain 813, it appears along with brief accounts of the teachings of other Zen masters including Shenhui, most likely source material for teaching and sermons. Two other copies (Pelliot tibétain 812 and 827) are hastily written and were probably copied down from oral or written sources by students. In all cases, it is clear that the texts attributed to Moheyan were popular but performed the same functions as many other texts found in the manuscripts. There is no sign that Moheyan or his works were afforded the preeminent historical importance given to them in the later Tibetan tradition and the recent academic study of Tibetan Zen.

Master Moheyan's Introduction to Instantaneous Meditation

The root of the worldly cycle of birth and death is the conceptualizing mind. Why is this? The movement of the conceptual mind is due to imprints that have always been present. You perceive in accordance with this movement, act in accordance with how you perceive, and achieve results in accordance with how you act. Thus everything from the heights of buddhahood to the depths of hell is projected by your own concepts, and that is all you ever see. On the other hand, if this mind does not arise, then it is impossible to hold on to as much as an atom of ordinary phenomena.

People who know that this is the way things are should renounce other activities, stay in just one place and no other, isolated and free from the hustle and bustle, and sit with crossed legs and a straight body, without sleeping from evening till dawn. When they engage in meditation, they should view their own mind. Since nothing exists there, they have no thoughts. If conceptual thoughts move, they should experience them. "How should we experience them?" Whatever thoughts arise should not be designated as moving or not moving. They should not be designated as existing or not existing. They should not be designated as virtuous or nonvirtuous. They should not be designated as afflicted or pure. They should not be designated as any kind of phenomenon at all.[16]

If the movement of mind is experienced in this way, it has no nature. This is called "practicing the dharma path." If the movement of mind is not experienced, or the experiences are false, then their cultivation will be pointless and they will remain ordinary people.

At first, when people who are new to cultivation view the mind, perceptions arise. They should apply the dharma explained above. After sitting for a long time, the mind will become stable and they will know that experience is itself conceptual thought. "How is that?" Due to the existence of a body, a shadow appears, and due to the appearance of the shadow, one knows that the body is there. Just so, experience arises due to the movement of thoughts, and due to the arising of experience, knowledge of experience arises. Then even that experience has no name or form. You cannot see a place where it came from in the beginning or determine to where it will go in the end. Experience and the place where experience occurs cannot be found by searching, and because it is inconceivable, it cannot be thought of. Not being attached even to the absence of thought is tathāgata meditation.

[*lacuna of one folio*]

Some say that it is not possible to engage in meditation without a method; so what meditation method should one practice? A person who has renounced all meditation sits in nonthought; this is the method by which one engages in meditation in the greater vehicle.[17]

Some think that this is a heretical meditation or something of the sort and are stricken with doubt. All heretics, since they depend on a view of a foundational self, accomplish both eternalism and nihilism at once. They do not say that the three realms are only mind, and for them there is no causation. Having come into contact with a master, they become fearful of perception and take pleasure in nothingness. Through contemplating this nothingness, they are born as formless gods. After many eons have passed, they think "this is not nirvāṇa," perceptions arise again, and they suddenly fall into hell. So there is a huge difference.

In addition, some wonder whether this is similar to the cessation meditation of the hearers. Though the contemplation of the hearers has many aspects, it is, in brief, based on the nonself of the person, the impermanence of all conditioned things, and . . .

[*lacuna of two folios*]

One should practice the six perfections by all means possible. If when sitting in meditation there are some imprints of dualistic concepts of stinginess and generosity, then the practice of the six perfections and meditation have become two different things, and as such should be abandoned. It is like the fact that the sun is equally obscured by both white and black clouds.

Basically there are three types of perfection: (i) this-worldly, (ii) transworldly, and (iii) supreme transworldly. The supreme perfection refers to a mind without apprehension or conceptualization that completes the six perfections in an instant. Otherwise, if you conceptualize and analyze dualities, then when you are sitting in meditation, you will be using awareness to suppress thought.

There are two aspects to the perfections: first, the practice of the perfections, which is the perfections as method; second, the nonmovement of internal thought, which is the perfections as insight. Thus, even if you do not appear to be overtly practicing the perfections, you may still possess the nature of the perfection of wisdom.

———

There are some who say that one should study extensively before entering into meditation. A so-called learned person may understand the nonarising of phenomena. A so-called learned person may be expert in verbal and written words, but he or she is not very learned. How is that so? You do not see the dharma by seeing. You do not hear the dharma by hearing. You do not experience the dharma through experience. You do not become conscious of the dharma through consciousness. Therefore, though you may search for something by sight, hearing, experience, and consciousness, you will not be seeking the dharma.

Though this is the essential teaching, there are those who have expressed doubts and disbelief. There are countless sentient beings who are unsuitable for this path, who don't understand the exhaustion of conceptual doubt, who are, in short, full of doubts and disbelief. They are deceived by their own concepts. Without having cultivated tathāgata meditation, they practice awareness and don't think of anything. In instantaneous tathāgata meditation, on the other hand, even when thoughts arise, you do not try to suppress the three spheres (of agent, action, and object). In this case, what need is there to talk of "meditation without error."

The lion cub brings terror to other animals even before it opens its eyes. The kalaviṅka bird comes to full development in the egg, and as soon as it breaks the egg, it can flap its wings. But it is not easy to find a metaphor for the qualities of meditation among worldly things, such is its effectiveness and benefit. This meditation requires effort in cultivating faith in the greater vehicle and belief that all phenomena are only mind. To desire something in the future without such cultivation is pointless, like constantly counting the wealth of a rich man without gaining any wealth of one's own.

Now a brief explanation of the method of cultivating the meaning of the Madhyamaka of the greater vehicle. In relative truth, all internal and external phenomena are from the beginning seen through the confusion of one's own conceptualization. And because they are dependently originated, having only the single feature of being illusory, in ultimate truth they are without substantiality. Because they are without substantiality, they are unarisen. Because they are unarisen, they are unceasing. Unarisen and unceasing, they are the space of reality. The space of reality is the dharmakāya. Since the nature of all phenomena is like this, one should cultivate not conceptualizing anything.

Question: When cultivating this, and concepts arise, what should I do?

Answer: This very mind that is without conceptualization is insubstantial, unarisen, unceasing, and identical with the space of reality. Since there is no need to fabricate it, do not chase after it or obstruct it. Instead, rest in primordial thusness without fabrication. How is this done? Since the mind is primordially nonabiding, it is unnecessary now to practice not abiding. Since the mind is primordially nonconceptual, it is unnecessary now to practice not conceptualizing. That would be to fabricate primordial thusness. This is also said in the sūtras:

Arising from phenomena without self,
Buddhas achieve perfect enlightenment.
Without conceptualization, without fixation,
They always cultivate this mind of enlightenment.[18]

And also from the sūtras:

Phenomena are the reflections of the mind;
Mind cannot itself be apprehended,
Unarisen, unceasing, beyond all mental activities,
Even and nonconceptual like the sky.

If you cultivate this, you will not remain in saṃsāra like a heretic. Endowed with means and wisdom, you will cleanse both the obscurations and the emotional afflictions. You will extend the two accumulations of merit and wisdom, and accomplish marvelous benefit for yourself and others. This is the body of merit. On the second bhūmi, you will attain the dharmakāya, and till the end of nonabiding nirvāṇa and saṃsāra, you will carry out the benefit of sentient beings.

A Summary of Master Moheyan's Introduction to Instantaneous Meditation

For those who are capable of it, there is *instantaneous entry,* also known as *the short path,* the *secret gate,* and *the gate to the path of liberation.* For those who are not capable, there are five methods. What are these five?

When you are resting in nonconceptualization:

1. If you experience the movements of the deluded mind, this is a neutral state.

2. If you experience the movements of the deluded mind and you follow that experience, this is the state of an ordinary sentient being.

3. If you experience the movements of the deluded mind and you understand that movement as a fault, then that experience will stop the various movements.

4. If you experience the movements of the deluded mind and know that they are without self, then this is one-sided peace, quiescent in emptiness.

5. If you experience the movements of the deluded mind and do not conceptualize or follow them, then each thought is liberated as soon as it comes. This is the correct meditation.

8

AUTHORITY AND PATRONAGE

THE TIBETAN EMPEROR AND THE KOREAN MONK

Though the narrative of the debate between Moheyan and the proponents of gradual practice dominated the later Tibetan picture of Zen, there is another story about Tibetan contact with Zen Buddhism. This story, also from the *Testimony of Ba,* is much more sympathetic toward Chinese Buddhism; however, later Tibetan historians paid scant attention to it. According to the *Testimony,* a Tibetan called Ba Sangshi traveled to China in the eighth century during the childhood of the Tibetan emperor Tri Song Detsen, in order to find a teacher to help establish Buddhism in Tibet. In Chengdu, he met Reverend Kim (684–762), one of the most famous Zen masters of the eighth century. Kim was a Korean monk, also known as Wuxiang, who had become the head of the Jingzhong temple in Sichuan. According to the *Testimony,* Kim gave advice and a prophecy about the success of Buddhism in Tibet to Ba Sangshi and the other Tibetans in his party, before they returned to Tibet.[1]

The *Testimony* shows at least that there was some contact at some point between the Tibetans and the lineage of Reverend Kim. Apart from his appearance in the *Testimony,* he is an entirely marginal figure in Tibet, and even his name was mangled in later versions of the *Testimony.* Whether he had any real influence on the early development of Tibetan Zen is unclear. The practices associated with Kim's lineage were vividly described in the *Record of the Dharma Jewel through the Generations* (hereafter the *Record*). These practices included mass ordinations into the lineage of the bodhisattva vow, performed at night and on ritual platforms.

Another source on Reverend Kim describes his meditation practice as the recitation of a single character in an increasingly low tone, ending in the silent state of nonthought.[2] The essence of Kim's instruction is supposed to be encapsulated in the "three phrases." The first two of these are no-recollection (*wuyi*) and no-thought (*wuxiang*). The third phrase is given differently in different sources, as either do not forget (*mowang*) or do not allow the unreal (*mowang*). According to Zongmi, the latter version was introduced by Kim's self-declared heir, Wuzhu, and indeed this is the phrase that is found in the *Record,* which was written by Wuzhu's disciples.[3]

Turning to the Tibetan Zen manuscripts, we find Kim among the masters quoted in Pelliot tibétain 116. The three phrases are not mentioned there; instead we have the following summary of Kim's teaching:

> When mind is in equanimity, all phenomena are equal. When you know perfection, there is no phenomenon that is not buddha. When you understand the meaning, mental states of attachment and desire do not arise. If you have experience of the perfect field of perception, there is nothing to look for. How is that? The suchness of the perfection of insight is primordial equality, and therefore it is not apprehended.[4]

The influence of Wuzhu and his disciples may have also had some influence on Tibetan Zen. Wuzhu's lineage, named Baotang after the temple in which he taught, is described in great detail in the *Record,* which claims Kim's lineage was passed on to Wuzhu despite the fact that the two never actually met. Though a Tibetan translation of this text has not emerged, brief accounts of Wuzhu's teachings appear once in the *Single Method* and twice in a compilation of masters' teachings in Pelliot tibétain 116 (see chapters 1 and 2). In the *Single Method,* Wuzhu is presented as saying: "Not thinking is discipline; not recollecting is concentration; the illusory mind not emerging is insight." This matches closely with Wuzhu's version of the three phrases presented in the *Record.*[5]

So, did Sichuan Zen lineages have a major influence on the Tibetan assimilation of Zen? Putting the story from the *Testimony* to one side, we know that the Tibetans conquered the kingdom of Nanzhou during the reign of Tri Song Detsen, in 762, giving them access to the Sichuan region. This would have made it possible for Tibetans to have come into contact with Chinese (or Korean) monks between this time and the fall of the empire in the mid-ninth century. Yet if there were any significant effects of that contact on Tibetan religion, there is little trace of them. Among the Dunhuang manuscripts, there are the few lines attributed to Kim and Wuzhu cited above and a very brief fragment of a story from the *Record,* about a conversation between the Zen patriarch Huiyuan and two Indian disciples of Bodhidharma, but that is all.[6]

These traces in the Dunhuang manuscripts probably came through contact with the same Chinese sources at Dunhuang. There are several copies of the *Record* in the original Chinese among the Dunhuang manuscripts; so there was no need to go as far as Sichuan to find sources to translate. So what about the Tibetan imperial interest in Zen at Dunhuang? We have already reviewed the conflicting and unreliable accounts of Tri Song Detsen's contacts with Moheyan. But there is another monk who is also said to have drawn the Tibetan emperor's attention.

PATRONAGE AT DUNHUANG

We do have some evidence of the interest of the Tibetan emperors in Chinese Buddhist literature in general, and Zen in particular. The *Twenty-Two Questions on the Greater Vehicle* was written by Tankuang, a Buddhist scholar monk and a Dunhuang resident for a royal patron. The treatise begins with an address to this patron:

> Having been lying on the sickbed for a lengthy period, I experienced serious pains and my health has deteriorated to such an extent that I am unable to undertake any travels. My loving thought runs to Your Majesty's countenance, although I lay suffering from an ailment on the frontier. It was a pleasant surprise to my mind and spirit when your thoughtful questions suddenly reached me.[7]

The ruler addressed here by Tankuang has been identified as Tri Song Detsen. If this is true, it is an interesting parallel to the story in the *Testimony* of the mission to Sichuan. It is not clear whether Tankuang should be seen as an exponent of Zen, however, though he did write a commentary to the *Vajracchedikā sūtra*. His other works, known mostly from the Dunhuang manuscripts, include *A Clarification of the Gradual Approach to Entering the Path of the Greater Vehicle*, a title that suggests a different approach than the authors of Zen treatises. Nevertheless, the treatise written for the emperor deals with many of the same issues that come up in Moheyan's *Ratification* and Kamalaśīla's *Stages of Meditation*, which shows that Tankuang was addressing the issues that were of concern to the Tibetan court in the late eighth century.

Several of the emperor's questions concern an issue addressed in many Zen texts: the difference between the approaches of the hearers, solitary buddhas, and bodhisattvas. In answer to a question about the nature of the enlightenment attained by these three types of practitioners, Tankuang explains the bodhisattva's enlightenment from the standpoint of the gradual and instantaneous approaches, without explicitly stating that one is better than the other. His explanation from the point of view of the instantaneous approach is as follows:

> A bodhisattva is in a position to comprehend that everything is empty and every dharma arises from the mind. If the mind is not agitated, everything is in a state of suchness; [the bodhisattva] is [therefore] able to give up a conceptualizing and grasping mind. The discriminating mind will not arise if the true features are understood. This is the wonderful principle of pure nirvāṇa.[8]

The treatise seems to have been written in the year 787, which would be in the immediate aftermath of the Tibetan conquest of Dunhuang, which the Tibetan army achieved after a decade-long siege. Given this fact, and the interest in Buddhism known to have been displayed by the Tibetan emperor at this time, it is possible that the twenty-two questions were indeed handed to Tankuang—by then in his early eighties—soon after the Tibetans finally took the city. So Tankuang's treatise may be an early example of an interest in Chinese Buddhist masters at the Tibetan

court. It certainly fits with Tri Song Detsen's project, stated in his own
edicts, and in Wangxi's *Ratification of the True Principle,* to establish
what would be considered an authentic and correct form of Buddhism
in Tibet. Equally, Tankuang's treatise suggests that there was no reason
for the Tibetans to equate Chinese Buddhism exclusively with Zen, or
the doctrines of instantaneous enlightenment.[9]

After the reign of Tri Song Detsen, patronage continued in the spon-
sorship of scholars translating Chinese Buddhist texts into Tibetan. By
the second quarter of the ninth century, there was a translation bureau at
Dunhuang headed by a monk known by both a Tibetan and a Chinese
name — to the Tibetans he was known as Chödrup, and to the Chinese,
Facheng. Some of his translations from Chinese, including a translation of the *Laṅkāvatāra sūtra,* were collected in the Tibetan canon. The
twentieth-century scholar Daishun Ueyama, who worked extensively
on the Dunhuang manuscripts related to Chödrup, believes that some
are written by the hand of the translator himself.[10] In any case, we have
in these manuscripts colophons attesting to the patronage Chödrup received from the Tibetan throne. The colophon to his translation of a
commentary on the *Laṅkāvatāra* reads:

> By the royal edict of the glorious divine Tsenpo, the great edi-
> tor-translator Go Chödrup translated, edited, and finalized this
> based on the Chinese book.[11]

As Chödrup was active during the middle of the ninth century, this
act of patronage probably dates from the 830s or 840s, shortly before
the end of Tibetan power in Dunhuang. As for the commentary on
the *Laṅkāvatāra,* though it did not survive in China, it is also found
in a Chinese version from Dunhuang (S.5603). In this manuscript, the
Chinese text of the commentary is accompanied by the root text written in Tibetan in red ink between the columns of Chinese characters.
Ueyama suggests that this manuscript was used by Chödrup while he
was working on his translation of the *Laṅkāvatāra.*[12]

Some of the other commentaries and original works by Chödrup
give us a picture of Tibetan interests in Chinese Buddhism in this period. Along with translations from the sūtra and dhāraṇī literature, we

have a translation of a text on the bodhisattva precepts and a number of texts composed by Chödrup himself, including a retelling of the story of Maudgalyāyana's trip to hell, a bilingual catechism on the view of the Madhyamaka, and a summary of the dharma compiled from scriptural sources. The last of these was requested by the Tibetan emperor, according to the colophon, which states that the text was written "due to the kindness of the Divine Son, the lord of men."[13]

Thus it is clear that patronage continued to be forthcoming from the Tibetan emperors in the first half of the ninth century for Buddhist translation and the composition of explanatory texts at Dunhuang. This evidence of imperial support for Chinese monks continuing right up to the end of the Tibetan empire belies the later Tibetan debate narratives that have Tri Song Detsen stating that Tibetan Buddhism will in the future be derived only from Indian sources.

THE ZEN BOOK

The text at the end of IOL Tib J 709, the compendium that begins with the treatise by Moheyan translated in the previous chapter, is called *The Zen Book*. The Tibetan word translated here as "book" is commonly found in the texts translated from Chinese to refer to an authoritative text. And instead of the later standard translation for "sūtra" (*mdo*), we have "dharma book" (*chos kyi yi ge*). Examples of this usage can be seen in the *Masters of the Laṅka,* which also quotes from a "worldly book" (*tha ma'i yi ge*). Underneath the title, the scribe has added a note saying, "The neck seal of the divine tsenpo Tri Song Detsen appears below." This statement implies that the text is a copy of an original (or a copy of a copy) to which the Tibetan emperor had affixed his "neck seal" (*mgur rgya*). Whether the name indicates a seal worn around the emperor's own neck, or (in another reading of *mgur*) "the seal of song" is unclear, but another Dunhuang manuscript, a description of Tibetan royal seals, makes it clear that this particular seal was considered to hold the highest authority.[14]

The opening lines of *The Zen Book* situate the work in a context that we are familiar with from the *Single Method,* the *Masters of the Laṅka,* and other Tibetan Zen works. The text is said to be intended for those practicing mahāyoga, identified as a teaching on tathāgata meditation, and located within the lineage of the *Laṅkāvatāra*. We already saw in chapter 3 the way that the term *mahāyoga* has been misunderstood in Zen texts as a reference to the tantric practices that had the same name. Here in *The Zen Book* we also see another term that in the later tradition is strongly associated with tantric practice: "commitments" (Tib. *dam tshig*, Skt. *samaya*). In tantric mahāyoga, the three main commitments are to venerate the master, to keep the teachings secret, and to avoid strife with fellow practitioners. These are not dissimilar to the commitments outlined here, which concern the Zen master (called the "master buddha") and the prohibitions on associating with those who do not follow the direct approach of Zen.

As with *mahāyoga,* we should not assume that the term *samaya* is a direct reference to the tantras, as the same term appears in the *Laṅkāvatāra*, in the phrase "the commitments of those who practice the greater vehicle." However, there is certainly more convergence in terminology between these Zen instructions and tantric practices than one might expect.[15]

The Zen Book closely paraphrases the third chapter of the *Laṅkāvatāra* in describing the hierarchy of meditation practice that culminates in tathāgata meditation. Thus the work is situating itself firmly within the authority of that sūtra, so it was probably written by someone who considered himself to be within the lineage of the *Laṅkāvatāra*. This would be quite possible if the text was written in the eighth century. Like many other Zen treatises, *The Zen Book* proceeds in a series of questions and answers, through which it becomes clear that the author is attempting to harmonize the positions of instantaneous and gradual practice:

> You must receive the esoteric instructions on the supreme wisdom. Those entering the great yoga first come to understand that all appearances are mind. Having understood that, they analyze all the positions, like whether nonsubstantial objects— which are the totally pure inner mind—arise from conditions and aggregations, or not. Or they make no effort at all.

This ambivalent answer seems to allow the possibility of both the gradual cultivation of insight through analysis and the path of nonaction. The latter is further explained in answer to the next question:

> This transcends the topics of all the philosophers. If you know that appearances are merely mind, this applies to all internal and external phenomena. The masters of this instantaneous approach to phenomena are not of one mind with the deluded, like ordinary folk, hearers, and heretics.

This explanation is very much in accord with the *Laṅkāvatāra,* which frequently points to the self-sufficient nature of the realization that appearances are merely mind. The next section of the text brings the gradual and instantaneous aspects of practice together with a simile that seems to be intended to convey the fact that skilled workers need to train at first to learn their skill, but after training, the skill becomes a part of what they are, and they need no further training. In the end, the author of *The Zen Book* seems to want to incorporate both approaches by suggesting that neither is sufficient on its own:

> Since it is important to train in the other stages, things like the eight meditations are not to be accomplished all at once; they are to be entered in succession. Purifying all the various concepts one by one is like trying to count all of the grains of sand on the earth; yet if one does not know what the essence of the mind is like, there will be no benefit from negating them instantaneously with a single antidote.

As in the simile of how ordinary people acquire and use their skills, this passage suggests again that a gradual training is required before the nature of the mind can be perceived. After training is complete it becomes effortless, and at this point, the single antidote (the realization of mind's nature) can be applied to all conceptualization. We might characterize this approach as gradual training followed by instantaneous realization. Was this an approach tailored to the approval of Tri Song Detsen? A parallel to the passage quoted here is found in the first text in IOL Tib J 710 (translated in chapter 3). This kind of intertextuality is too common for any firm conclusions to be drawn, but it is possible that *The Zen Book* was put together from already existent sources as an introduction to Zen for the Tibetan emperor.

The arguments outlined earlier for dating Pelliot tibétain 116 also apply here, and there is no reason not to place the manuscript containing *The Zen Book*, IOL Tib J 709, in the tenth century. But we must
distinguish between the dates of the manuscripts and the dates of the
texts they contain. In the case of those Tibetan Zen texts that have been
identified as translations from the Chinese, the original works are from
no later than the early ninth century. This is in accord with other aspects
of Tibetan Buddhism at Dunhuang; tantric texts seem to have become
widely popular only after the end of the Tibetan empire, but they continued to be based on works translated during the Tibetan empire, heed-
less of the later developments in Buddhist tantra going on in India.[16]

It seems that something similar occurred with Tibetan Zen. The major
translations were all done during the imperial period, but the texts continued to be written down into the tenth century. Evidence for the existence of *The Zen Book* in the imperial period may be found in a Tibetan
monastic library catalog from the early eighth century, the *Lhan kar ma*.
This text is an invaluable source of information for determining which
texts of Buddhist literature were translated into Tibetan in the imperial
period. It is organized thematically, and the section that concerns us is
headed "Zen books" (*bsam gtan gi yi ge*). In this case, we should probably
translate *bsam gtan* more generally as "meditation." They are:

Three Stages of Meditation, by Kamalaśīla
Stages of Meditation, by Vajrakīrti
Stages of Meditation, by Yeshe Nyingpo
Meditation on the Mind of Enlightenment, by Gyalwa Ö
Meditation on the Mind of Enlightenment, by Mañjuśrīmitra
Showing the Gate to Meditation, by Kalyāṇavarman
Stages of Meditation, by Dharmamati
The Zen Book, by Bodhidharmatāra, translated from the Chinese[17]

The last book in this list bears the same title as the text translated
here, and the ascription to Bodhidharma confirms that it was considered
a Zen text.[18] The catalog indicates that it was a fairly long text (in nine
hundred verses), but since the text in IOL Tib J 709 seems to be incomplete, this is not problematic. On the other hand, the title "Zen book"

may be intended generically, as it is in the title of this group of texts. When we turn to the other texts in the group, it is clear that most are not Zen texts; in fact, five of the eight are treatises on graduated meditation practice by Indian masters. The text called *Meditation on the Mind of Enlightenment* by Mañjuśrīmitra is an early Great Perfection (*rdzogs chen*) work.

The *Lhan kar ma* shows that when the library catalog was compiled in the early ninth century, Chinese Zen texts were placed in the same genre as other instructional texts on meditation, including the more scholastically inclined and strongly gradualist Indian texts and the tantric-flavored poetry of early Dzogchen. According to the narrative of the debate, this was after the Chinese teaching was banned in Tibet, yet here there is no sign of any sense of conflict between instantaneous and gradual approaches, or between Chinese and Indian sources. The presence of a work by Kamalaśīla in the same library category as *The Zen Book* fits much better with the brief account from the *Lamp for the Eyes of Contemplation* mentioned in chapter 6, in which Moheyan and Kamalaśīla are both said to have taught in Tibet, but no strife between them or their followers is mentioned.

THE GLAMOUR OF EMPIRE

We have seen that Tri Song Detsen and other Tibetan emperors did patronize Chinese Buddhist teachers, including Zen monks. Yet the scribe who wrote "The neck seal of the divine tsenpo Tri Song Detsen appears below" was probably not doing so to offer a bit of historical trivia to readers of the manuscript. In line with our aim to understand the use and function of manuscripts, we should consider what the purpose of making this assertion might have been. The manuscript containing *The Zen Book* is quite different from the comparably large compendium Pelliot tibétain 116. In fact there is no overlap in the texts they contain at all. This suggests that they were created for quite different functions. The arrangement of texts alongside *The Zen Book* in this manuscript is as follows:[19]

> *Introduction to Instantaneous Meditation* by Moheyan
> A treatise entitled *Showing Faults in Meditation*

A dialogue between Brahma and Mañjuśrī on various topics
Questions and answers on aspects of meditation
The teachings of the master Bodhināgendra
A treatise on *śamatha* and *vipaśyanā*
A treatise on means and wisdom
Teachings on Madhyamaka by the master Haklenayaśas
The Zen Book

As I suggested in the previous chapter, these texts do not suggest a particular ritual practice but could have been sources for teaching and sermons. Another possibility, given the careful production that clearly went into this manuscript, is that it was created as a prestige object, to be owned and venerated by a teacher or patron of a Tibetan Zen lineage. This would explain the placing of a major text by Moheyan at the beginning and a text with the Tibetan emperor's personal seal of approval at the end.

The invocation of the authority of the Tibetan empire, and the emperor Tri Song Detsen in particular, is a central feature of the later Tibetan "treasure" (*gter ma*) tradition. From its beginnings in the eleventh century onward, the key imperial figure changed from being Tri Song Detsen to the tantric adept Padmasambhava, though the emperor played an important role throughout the tradition. The preeminent role of Tri Song Detsen as an emblem of the glamour of the Tibetan empire is also apparent in some of the Dunhuang manuscripts. He plays a central role in early historical narratives of the introduction of Buddhism to Tibet, such as the fragment of the *Testimony of Ba* and a narrative of how the *Prayer of Excellent Conduct* came to be practiced in Tibet. He is also invoked in verses extolling the virtues of the Buddhist emperors of Tibet.[20]

Thus, whether or not *The Zen Book* was compiled for Tri Song Detsen, and whether original copies were stamped with his personal seal, the statement in the manuscript here serves mainly to infuse the text, and by extension the whole compendium, with the glamour and authority of the Tibetan empire. This was done through making a direct connection between the original text (of which this is a copy) and the action of the emperor in approving the teachings of Zen Buddhism presented as they are here. Connecting the past to the present in this way directly affects practice, through lending authority to the texts supporting ritual practice, teaching, and the transmission of lineage, and through providing models for contemporary patrons to support these practices.

The Zen Book

––––––––––

The neck-seal of the divine emperor Tri Song Detsen appears below.

This is intended for those entering the great yoga. The tathāgatas taught innumerable gates to meditation. From among them, there are the meditations with coarse attributes of the hearers and the extremists; the stages of meditation with and without focus points of the bodhisattvas endowed with faith and those who reside on the bhūmis; and tathāgata meditation, beyond all extremes. Within the latter meditation, there is a distinction into three types: worldly, transworldly, and supreme transworldly. Among these meditations, tathāgata meditation is the best. Thus it is said in the transmission of the noble *Laṅkāvatāra*.

Therefore without speaking of the attributes of the other types, I will teach how great yogins may cultivate the transmission of tathāgata meditation, day and night.

"How does mind come into being?"

You must receive the esoteric instructions on the supreme wisdom. Those entering the great yoga first come to understand that all appearances are mind. Having understood that, they analyze all the positions, like whether nonsubstantial objects—which are the totally pure inner mind—arise from conditions and aggregations, or not. Or they make no effort at all.

"Why is that?"

This transcends the topics of all the philosophers. If you know that appearances are merely mind, this applies to all internal and external phenomena. The masters of this instantaneous approach to phenomena are not of one mind with the deluded, like ordinary folk, hearers, and heretics. So, having developed the awakening mind in that way, you bring sentient beings to maturity; but even while doing this, it is all merely your own mind. These great yogins do not carry out strenuous activities. It is like, for example, training for a worldly livelihood. At first, those people who rely on a particular skill accomplish specific methods that determine how to act with respect to jewels, or seeds, or milk. Just so, those sons who pursue tathāgata meditation abide in the bliss of self-referential awareness, the noble supreme wisdom that is not mind, or ego, or the ego-consciousness. They do not accomplish it from a cause, and it is definitely not an effect. It is the activity by which you become a buddha of reality itself. After that, they do not descend to other levels, like those of the heretics or hearers.

"How does one receive the commitments?"

One who has previously made offerings to many buddhas and has pure aspirations must rely on the master-buddha, and upon no other. They are not to study the various terminologies for designation with the deluded who mentally engage with unborn and unobstructed phenomena.

"Why is that?"

Since the meditations of the other vehicles, which are based on practicing inner subjugation, have no power in themselves to bring about the great benefit of sentient beings, they are not sufficient. Among those whose meditation is based on apprehension, even if they have achieved special powers, their own supreme wisdom is darkened by their obscurations. Even if they have purified these a little bit, they are far from realization.

Since it is important to train in the other stages, things like the eight meditations are not to be accomplished all at once; they are to be entered in succession. Purifying all the various concepts one by one is like trying to count all of the grains of sand on the earth. Yet if one does not know what the essence of the mind is like, there will be no benefit either from negating them instantaneously with a single antidote.

9

FUNERALS AND MIRACLES

LIVES, DEATHS, AND MIRACLES

In Chinese and Tibetan Buddhist traditions, stories about the deaths of famous masters play a significant role in lineage histories. These stories are often accompanied by material culture, especially portraits of the master, either paintings or statues, and sometimes the mummified remains of the body itself. These objects served as the focus for devotional practices aimed at the masters of the lineage. The practices could include recitation of prayers to the lineage masters, and in the later Tibetan tradition, forms of "guru yoga" involving visualization of the deceased masters.

Thus the practices that support and ratify a lineage, focused as they are on figures who have passed away, are inseparably bound up with death. The manuscript Pelliot tibétain 996 contains a series of narratives that show us how death and the rituals around it were part of Zen practice. Pelliot tibétain 996 is a compilation of a series of texts relating to a lineage that began in Central Asia and ended up in Amdo (modern Qinghai province). The first text tells the stories of the Indian Zen master Artanhwer, his Chinese disciple Busing, and the latter's disciple Man Heshang. The next text is about Man's Tibetan disciple Tsigtsa Namkai Nyingpo and is followed by one of the latter's poems. The final text is about another Tibetan, Pug Yeshe Yang, and an important work he composed, called *Drawn from Eighty Sutras*. The lineage does not overlap with any other known Zen lineages, and the compiler of these texts made no attempt to trace the lineage back beyond Artanhwer to Bodhidharma or any other Indian teacher.[1]

There is some evidence in the Tibetan Zen materials, however, that this is not a completely isolated lineage. The *Single Method* (translated in chapter 1) cites the following masters in this order: (i) Nāgārjuna, (ii) Bodhidharmatāra, (iii) Wuzhu, (iv) Xiangmo Zang, (v) Artanhwer, (vi) Wolun, (vii) Moheyan, (viii) Āryadeva. This is a nonchronological mixed bag of Zen masters, bracketed between the famous Madhyamaka exegetes Nāgārjuna and his disciple Āryadeva. It seems to be a presentation of masters who were important to the lineages practiced at Dunhuang in a way that validates them in the tradition of Madhyamaka (on the role of Madhyamaka in Tibetan Zen, see chapter 5). The actual teaching attributed to Artanhwer is this: "Whatever you experience in the mind, that is the definitive path of yoga."

The text in Pelliot tibétain 996 is divided into four parts. The first describes "the lineage of spiritual guides of the master Namkai Nyingpo." It begins with a description of how this lineage was brought from India to Central Asia, along the northern Silk Route:

> The master Artanhwer, an instructor who knew the path of the sameness of all phenomena, traveled to Anxi from India, for the sake of sentient beings. There he gathered three hundred students and taught them how to enter the greater vehicle. He received divine food offerings from the sky, which satiated his three hundred students.

After this brief account of the master's achievements, the text turns to the miraculous events surrounding his death:

> At over a hundred years old, he passed away in the posture of nirvāṇa. Then the king of Anxi struck the body and said, "If the master came to explain the dharma to multitudes of sentient beings, why did he teach only a few words?" And after a while the master rose again for three days and taught the dharma to the king of Anxi, Kuatsi Wang.

The spelling of this master's name (*a rtan hwer*) suggests that it has been rendered into Tibetan from Chinese characters that were attempting to transliterate a foreign name. One scholar has argued that it represents the Persian name Ardašīr, though this is difficult to substantiate. The first part of the name may represent the Chinese surname An, which would imply an origin in the region of Sogdiana. In any case, the lineage is first recorded in Anxi, the name of the Chinese command center for its western territories. This had been in Kucha until the late 680s, when Kucha was taken by the Tibetan army, and the Chinese moved the Anxi commandery to Qocho. Thus by the time of Artanhwer, Anxi may have referred to Qocho (Ch. Gaochang).[2]

With the next stage in the lineage, we have a Chinese master, Busing, who was based in Dunhuang and the surrounding region. Again, the description of the master's life is brief, and is followed by a more detailed account of his death:

When he was eighty, a five-colored cloud appeared to the west of his monastery in the Suzhou region and stopped above the Heshang's head. Then, seated without moving in meditation posture, the Heshang left this life, and the cloud returned to the west. Then for three days the land remained in darkness, changing the colors of the grass and trees.

This and the other texts in Pelliot tibétain 996 present the reader with a combination of facts about the movements and patronage of the lineage masters and miraculous occurrences at the time of their death. The only master whose death is not described is Busing's student Man Heshang. The latter is unknown to the later Zen tradition but was obviously well regarded in Dunhuang, where his *Words on Understanding the Nature* are found in several manuscripts. The preface to this poetic work refers to him as "a Zen Master from Chongji monastery." Man Heshang's death does not feature here because he leaves for China, and is out of the purview of the text. This strongly suggests that the text was composed in the Amdo region.[3]

SACRED GEOGRAPHY

The deaths of two further masters, Namkai Nyingpo and Yeshe Yang, are described in similar terms. In each case, miraculous clouds or lights, usually of five colors, appear and then disappear toward the west. These clouds of five colors are mentioned in works on the Chinese divination method of examining the shapes and colors of clouds and vapors. The five colors are green/blue, red, yellow, white, and black. And the shape of the cloud along with the predominant color indicates the result of the divination. The following example is taken from a Dunhuang manuscript:

> Whenever a five-colour vapor is seen above someone's house and it remains there steadily during the last days of the month, ... if [the vapor above] the house has mostly greenish-blue, this is the vapor of a dead body; if mostly red, it is the vapor of gold and jade; if mostly yellow, this house will go through extensive renovation works; if mostly white, this land has copper and iron; if mostly black, this house will serve as the abode of the divine spirit (*shen*).[4]

This seems to be the cultural context for the five-colored clouds of Pelliot tibétain 996, though there is also a parallel in the Indian tantric tradition of associating five colored lights with the five buddhas, and in the later Tibetan Nyingma tradition, of the dissolution of the body of an adept into five colored lights.[5] Here in Pelliot tibétain 996, the theme of the cloud, or light, disappearing to the west indicates an additional influence from the "pure land" sūtras and the devotional practices surrounding them, generally directed toward the buddha Amitābha and his pure land of Sukhāvatī, located in the west. The popular cult of Amitābha and his western pure land was present in Dunhuang, as we know from the many copies of prayer and eulogies dedicated to the theme in Chinese and Tibetan.[6]

By the end of the narratives in Pelliot tibétain 996, the lineage has moved into the Tibetan region of Amdo (in modern Qinghai). This area became a thriving hub of monastic Tibetan Buddhism during the first half of the eighth century. Pelliot tibétain 996 mentions some of the key sites in this region, including the cities of Tsongka and Anchung, and the retreat center of Triga. Several other Dunhuang manuscripts mention Tibetan religious establishments in this area, including a set of letters of passage that belonged to a Chinese pilgrim who passed through in the tenth century. Moreover, it is in this same area that the Tibetan monastic code was preserved after the fall of the Tibetan empire. In the later Tibetan historical tradition, a monk called Gewa Rabsel is credited with preserving the monastic ordination tradition during Tibet's age of political fragmentation in this very area. According to one source, Gewa Rabsel is said to have built a stūpa in the nearby Dantig valley in order to ward off the advances of yogins teaching the instantaneous approach to enlightenment. As this seems to have been a thriving region for monastic Buddhism, it is quite plausible that there were tensions and competition in the establishment of new Buddhist lineages here.[7]

In this context, we can understand why the narrative in Pelliot tibétain 996 is particularly concerned to describe the sites and miraculous circumstances of the deaths and funerals of its lineage masters. By linking these miraculous events with the regions and temples in which they occurred, the narrative embeds the lineage in a sacred geography. This creates a structure for further practices, such as regular rituals and pilgrimage. We can see in the course of reading Pelliot tibétain 996 how the lineage it describes moves into new areas, and how these areas are made sacred to the lineage by the narratives around the masters' deaths. What would follow, were the lineage to be successful, is the sequence of regular practices that maintain and protect the right of the holders of this lineage to the temples and the region to which they have staked their claim.

ZEN AND TANTRA

The second text in Pelliot tibétain 996 is dedicated to a teacher called Namkai Nyingpo, a student of Man Heshang who is said to have become a monk during the reign of Tri Song Detsen (that is, in the second half of the eighth century). Though he is known in this text as Tsigtsa Namkai Nyingpo, he might be identical with the contemporaneous figure Nub Namkhai Nyingpo, celebrated in Tibetan histories as a disciple of the tantric master Padmasambhava and an adept in the tantric practices of mahāyoga. While there is no other evidence for this identification, it is striking that the next figure in the lineage, Pug Yeshe Yang, is also known as one of Padmasambhava's students.

As with the previous masters, except for Man Heshang, more than half of the biography of Namkai Nyingpo is concerned with his death and the miracles surrounding it. This is followed by a poem attributed to him, titled *Praise for the Path of Yoga*. The presence of terminology drawn from the tantras is unmistakable here—the maṇḍala of the vajra-dhātu, bodhicitta, mūdra, and the characterization of realization as "the supreme siddhi." All of this, especially the allusion to the vajradhātu maṇḍala, points to an association with the tantric literature of the yoga class, such as the *Sarvatathāgata-tattvasaṃgrāha*.

Other parts of Namkai Nyingpo's poem are drawn from the Zen tra-dition, like the image of a bird flying in the sky, which also appears in the teaching attributed to Shenhui in Pelliot tibétain 116 (see chapter 2). The way these verses weave together this material suggests an audience familiar with both Zen discourses and tantric practices. This is the gen-eral situation that Nub Sangye Yeshe was fighting to change in his *Lamp for the Eyes of Contemplation*. In chapter 10, we will look at how Zen and tantra were integrated in specific practices.

PATRONS AND TEXTS

The last text in Pelliot tibétain 996 is on Pug Yeshe Yang. He is said to have received support from a member of the influential Dro clan, in this case a monk called Dro Śākya. This is not the only instance of this clan's being linked to Zen. Earlier in this lineage, the Chinese monk Man Heshang is said to have received patronage from a Tibetan minister by the name of Tri Sumje. This is almost certainly the well-known Tibetan from the Dro clan, Tri Sumje Tagnang, who as commander-in-chief of the Tibetan army played a major role in negotiating the Sino-Tibetan peace accord in the early 820s. Before this, in the first decade of the ninth century, he lived at Dunhuang, where he sponsored the construction of a Buddhist temple.[8]

In addition, as we saw in chapter 7, the preface to the *Ratification* mentions that the queen who invited the Zen master Moheyan to Tibet was from the Dro clan. Other followers of Moheyan mentioned there are members of the Nanam and Nyang clans. As Paul Demiéville pointed out, the reason that the Dro clan in particular features among the patrons of Zen may be their role, in the latter part of the eighth century, as the custodians of Tibet's northeast frontier with China.

According to Pelliot tibétain 996, Pug Yeshe Yang wrote a treatise showing that the words of the Zen masters of India, China, and Tibet were in accord with the sūtras. This work is known by two titles: *Drawn from Eighty Sutras* and *Essential Points in the Cultivation of the Great Yoga.* Here the first title is only suggested, but the description of the text and a brief précis of its contents allow us to identify it. This was one of the most popular Tibetan texts written in the Zen idiom, found not only in manuscripts from Dunhuang but also in manuscripts from Tabo and Gondlha at the other extreme of the Tibetan cultural area, far to the west. The text itself is similar to the *Single Method* and other Zen question and answer texts (see chapter 1), though its answers are for the most part restricted to quotes from the sūtras, without any commentary. The concerns of *Drawn from Eighty Sutras* are also similar to other Tibetan Zen texts; many of the questions are about the single method (*tshul gcig*) and its place in the Buddhist doctrine of the greater vehicle.[9]

Thus, as well as laying a claim for its lineage in the sacred geography of the Amdo region, the narratives in Pelliot tibétain 996 also function as a preface for a text that, like the *Single Method,* defends the validity of the Zen approach within the orthodox positions of greater vehicle Buddhism. This is a mutually supportive relationship: the narratives with their tales of miraculous deaths defend the validity of the lineage that produced *Drawn from Eighty Sutras,* while the text defends the authenticity of the teachings that are transmitted by the lineage. It would be perhaps too restrictive to suggest one particular use for the manuscript Pelliot tibétain 996. It was carefully written in a rather idiosyncratic hand not seen in any of the other Dunhuang manuscripts and may therefore have been brought to Dunhuang from one of the temples in Amdo mentioned in the narrative. As we have seen, the texts in the manuscript could also have been a source to be drawn upon in the teaching and practice of the rituals associated with the lineage. The manuscript could also have been a sacred object in itself for a member of this lineage, serving as a token for membership of the lineage, just as some of the manuscript copies of the *Platform Sutra* were used for this purpose.[10]

A Brief Teaching on the Lineage of Spiritual Guides of the Master Namkai Nyingpo

The master Artanhwer, an instructor who knew the path of the sameness of all phenomena, traveled to Anxi from India, for the sake of sentient beings. There he gathered three hundred students and taught them how to enter the greater vehicle. He received divine food offerings from the sky, which satiated his three hundred students. At over a hundred years old, he passed away in the posture of nirvāṇa. Then the king of Anxi struck the body and said, "If the master came to explain the dharma to multitudes of sentient beings, why did he teach only a few words?" And after a while the master rose again for three days and taught the dharma to the king of Anxi, Kuatsi Wang.

Of the eight students who understood his dharma, the best was Busing Heshang. He traveled to Shazhou and Ganzhou, teaching many students. He received a divine feast from the sky, which satiated his students. When he was eighty, a five-colored cloud appeared to the west of his monastery in the Suzhou region and stopped above the Heshang's head. Then, seated without moving in meditation posture, the Heshang left this life, and the cloud returned to the west. Then for three days the land remained in darkness, changing the colors of the grass and trees.

Of the eight students who understood his dharma, the best was Man Heshang. He was offered a divine feast, which allowed him to conquer sleep, meditating constantly day and night. He went to Tsongka, where he taught the dharma to many students. When he bestowed meditation instructions, his student Tsigtsa Namkai understood his meaning. The

Heshang also taught the path of seeing.[11] At the age of thirty, he went to China. The minister Zhang Trisumje Marbu offered the Heshang edible tributes, which he repaid by offering a gift. When the Heshang was leaving, Trisumje asked him, "Who is able to teach the dharma path?" He replied, "My student Tsigtsa Namkai knows the meaning of the dharma. Because he is able to teach the path, those who practice the dharma path turn to him." After this, he went to China.

A Brief Account of the Qualities of the Master Namkai Nyingpo

Namkai Nyingpo was first ordained as a monk during the lifetime of the Tsenpo Tri Song Detsen. He took his monastic vows in the monastery, made alms-rounds, and so on. He took a vow to remain in the good qualities of recitation, and from the meditation master Man Heshang he learned the instantaneous approach to the meaning of the greater vehicle. Meditating on this, he understood the meaning of the dharma. Then he made this prophecy:

> The child of the lion is like a fox. My master was like that in relation to Busing Heshang, and I as a student was like that in relation to him. But sometimes the child of the fox is a lion. The relationship between me as a master and you as my students will be like that.

Thus he greatly praised them.

When the teacher Namkai Nyingpo made offerings to the statue at Triga that naturally emerges from a tree, light emanated from it. Later, when he was living in the retreat center of Yamyog, there were miraculous signs including the passing over of a five-colored cloud. One day, when he was practicing the dharma path and had just completed his vow to abide in the good qualities of recitation (he was seventy-one, and it was the twenty-ninth day of spring in the year of the dog, and he was at the Zhongpong hermitage), he sat cross-legged and unmoving, and passed away, without any change in his complexion. That night, in the middle of the sky between the mountain range of Zhongpong that extends below the retreat center and Mount Srinpo, two great streams of light emerged and lit up the whole of the countryside before disappearing into the west.

Similar things were seen by many people, including two monks of Byilig called Tamje Palgi Gyaltsen and Gwen Lodrö. At the end of the week-long funeral, five hundred gods and humans requested a teaching, and offered prayers. As a result, at midnight, light appeared from the retreat of Tagsa Dragtsa and disappeared into the west.

"Praise for the Path of Yoga"
by the Master Namkai Nyingpo

Nonabiding, equality: this is the path of ultimate yoga,
Unchanging, unproduced, and unceasing from the start.
That which appears is like a bird's path through the sky:
Impossible to objectify it with a view or express it in words.

Those noble beings with the wisdom-mind of intrinsic awareness,
Understand and master this freedom from objectifying concepts.
Homage to the treasury of the tathāgatas themselves,
The tradition that is the source of noble beings.

The path of great sages is in equality from the beginning,
The maṇḍala of nonobjectification and sameness.
Equalization without arising or cessation
Is the wisdom of the Vajradhātu.

Those who have mastered bodhicitta
Can perform the summoning of an immovable mind.
The mūdra that liberates the children of the Conqueror,
Is the supreme form, sameness itself; to cultivate it
Is to be the dharmakāya, complete and perfect.
This is what we call the supreme accomplishment.

Pug Yeshe Yang

This greater vehicle path of nonconceptual meditation was also taught and summarized by the monk Pug Yeshe Yang. He took ordination during the reign of the ancestral kings and studied the dharma in a dharma college.[12] Relying on the transmissions and instructions of his spiritual guide and his own personal experience, he stayed in the monastery and for fifty years undertook the mode of meditation that is without abiding or conceptualizing. As a result, he comprehended the meaning of nonabiding.

He comprehended the definitive meanings of the sūtras and found that they agreed with the transmissions and instructions of his virtuous friends and his own meditation experience. Drawing on the transmissions and instructions of the experienced Zen masters of India, China, and Tibet, and their sources in the statements from the greater vehicle sūtras of definitive meaning, he composed 108 sections comprising questions regarding doubts, with citations from eighty sūtras, two or three sūtra citations for each and every doubt.

All the buddhas of the three times attain nirvāṇa through the single gate of the greater vehicle. Yet it is said that one thousand years after the nirvāṇa of Śākyamuni Buddha, nobody will meditate on the single-taste ultimate truth, engaging instead in mere texts and words; quarrels and fights will develop, and the saṅgha will split into five communities. If this is so, what happens to the essence of the greater vehicle: nonapprehension and the single method?

Though this method can be seen in the instructions of many virtuous friends and passages from the profound sūtras, in order to assist the three levels of people, five types of meaning are taught to beginners.[13] These are (i) the single method of the greater vehicle, (ii) the nature of the single method and the means of cultivating it, (iii) the errors of nonconceptualization in the single method and the qualities of cultivating it, (iv) the qualities of cultivating it, and (v) the result: the three kāyas and nirvāṇa. The essence of this is that without cultivation it is very difficult to understand the words. But with cultivation comes experience, and then one can understand and teach the meaning of those words.[14]

At the age of eighty, on the dawn of the eighth day of the autumn month, in the year of the horse, the master of meditation that encompasses all of the above, Pug Yeshe Yang, passed away without agitation, in the retreat of Tsigtsa Namkai Nyingpo in Triga Mong Yogda.[15] Afterward, his disciples performed meritorious deeds in the temple of Ngatse. Then the corpse was escorted with parasols and carried to the retreat in Anchung by people of the surrounding region. On that day a cloud of five colors appeared above Triga castle and was seen by all of the local people and herdsmen.

When the corpse was conveyed to the region of Anchung, escorted by the monk Dro Śākya and others, it was brought to the peak of Mount Sinpo, and a five-colored cloud appeared in the sky and formed into a mist. While they were taking it to the Anchung retreat, the five-colored cloud came from the sky to the peak of the mountain and remained there until their arrival.

ZEN AND TANTRA

ZEN IN TANTRIC PRACTICE

The anonymous author of a tenth-century treatise on the tantric practices of mahāyoga makes the following statement about the "view," or philosophical background to practice: "According to the texts of Zen, Sutra, and Mantra, the view is nonapprehension."[1] What is interesting about this statement is not so much whether it is true, though it is true that the phrase "nonapprehension" can be found in sutric and tantric literature as well as in Zen texts, but that there was apparently no controversy in making such a statement. The context of the statement does not suggest any firm doctrinal or sectarian distinctions to defend or overcome. And if this shared view is not perceived as a problem, then there may not have been any perceived barriers to engaging in the practices of these different approaches. Recent studies of Chinese Zen suggest that this was the case and that there was a great deal of overlap between Zen and esoteric Buddhism during the eighth to tenth centuries.

During the eighth century, the Indian masters Śubhākarasiṃha and Vajrabodhi gave teachings in China to students from a variety of different backgrounds, including Zen lineages, and some of these students were involved in the establishment of ordination platforms, including one with the tantric title "Five Buddha Perfect Awareness Platform." There is evidence in the Chinese Dunhuang manuscripts that this trend continued through to the tenth century. The eighty-seven-panel concertina manuscript Pelliot chinois 3913 is a compilation serving as a manual for entering the maṇḍala of the buddha Vairocana. The text gives two lineages of transmission for its teachings, and these are both unmistakably lists of Zen teachers. The title of the work implies that it is intended for a ritual on an ordination platform, suggesting that the ordination platform used in Zen rituals could be regarded as a physical representation of the tantric maṇḍala.[2] It is not very useful to call this "syncretism," a term implying the conjoining of two distinct entities. Rather, what we are seeing is the transmission of texts and teaching lineages without the firm distinctions imposed by the later traditions.[3]

The text translated here is from Pelliot tibétain 699, one of five closely related manuscripts, all apparently written by the same person: Pelliot tibétain 322, 626, 634, 699, and 808. The first of these is a prayer to the tantric deities of the Illusion Web (*māyājāla*) tantras, the second and third are tantric practice texts (*sādhana*), the fourth is a commentary on a brief Zen practice text, and the fifth offers Zen interpretations of Buddhist concepts like the three jewels.[4]

The striking feature of the two sādhanas in Pelliot tibétain 626 and 634 is that they incorporate the techniques of observing the mind found in Tibetan Zen texts, especially those attributed to Moheyan (see chapters 6 and 7). Meditation in mahāyoga sādhanas tends to be laid out in three phases known as the three concentrations (Tib. *ting nge 'dzin*, Skt. *samādhi*), and this is what we see in Pelliot tibétain 626 and 634. These three are: (i) the concentration on suchness, (ii) the concentration on total illumination, and (iii) the concentration on the cause.[5] It is in the first of these that we find the technique of observing the mind described:

> Regarding the phrase *observing the mind:* the method is to observe one's own mind, and the knowledge is to neither abide in nor conceptualize it. *Not being anything* means settling the mind, which is taught in two methods: the method for examining the mind, and the method for settling. Regarding the method for examining: to look at the mind with the mind is a method for realizing that the entity mind is without any color or shape whatsoever. Regarding the method for settling: one should settle the mind without thinking of anything.[6]

The mental state resulting from this concentration is described in these two sādhanas in terms of nonthought (*mi bsam*), nonconceptualization (*mi rtog*), and not engaging the mind (*yid la mi byed pa*), a triad similar to the "three phrases" of Reverend Kim and Wuzhu (see chapter 8). The resulting state of mindfulness is also described using a series of metaphors, like that of the watchman spotting a thief, many of which are drawn from the works of Shenxiu, and were also used by Moheyan.[7]

The two sādhanas show that the contemplative techniques taught under the heading of "observing the mind," which were popular in Chinese and Tibetan Zen lineages at Dunhuang, including that of Moheyan, were adapted to the first phase of mahāyoga meditation practice. These sources, and the verses attributed to Namkai Nyingpo discussed in chapter 9, strongly suggest that the context for the practice of meditation instructions from Zen lineages was often a tantric one. Since by the tenth century, mahāyoga had become the most popular form of tantric Buddhism in Tibet, it is not surprising that mahāyoga sādhanas became one of the main settings for these Zen meditation practices.

THE BRIEF PRECEPTS AND COMMENTARY

The text that is the subject of the commentary in Pelliot tibétain 699 is a brief series of meditation instructions. It not named, but is quoted in the Zen chapter of the *Lamp for the Eyes of Contemplation* under the title *Brief Precepts* (*Lung chung*). It also appears in other Dunhuang manuscripts: in a dedicated manuscript, IOL Tib J 689; in the compilation of Zen texts, Pelliot tibétain 21, that also contains the Madhyamaka-themed texts translated in chapter 5; and in a small concertina manuscript, IOL Tib J 1774, where it is followed by some notes on the tantras. This is enough to suggest that this brief text was quite popular, probably because of its unusually detailed and specific instructions on meditation in the Zen style.[8]

After an evocation of the compassionate motivation to end the suffering of all sentient beings, the *Brief Precepts* gives instructions on the practice of meditation, beginning with observing the mind, and moving on to a state of neither thinking nor conceptualizing. It then describes the resulting realization of emptiness and the equality of saṃsāra and nir-vāṇa, from which the mind is liberated of itself with no need to suppress concepts. The meditator is instructed to remain in an unmoving state of concentration, while the meditative experience becomes increasingly subtle, peaceful, and clear.

The commentary explains the practice of meditation at some length, in the most involved instructions on the practice of looking at one's mind found in any of the Tibetan Zen texts. This process is an intel-lectual inquiry, similar to the way it is described in Pelliot tibétain 626 and 634, but in much greater detail. The inquiry is based on asking eight questions about the mind:

> These eight questions about the mind are to be used deductively
> to come to a conclusion. Is the mind an apprehended object?
> Is it permanent? Is it transitory? Is it created? Is it terminated?
> Does it have the four colors? Does it have the eight shapes? Is it
> a knower?

Answering these questions leads to the conclusion that one's mind is not located anywhere, and this clears the way for a state of nonthought and nonconceptualization. The commentary also uses the three phrases, here explicitly named: no-thought (*mi sems*), no-recollection (*mi dran*), and illusoriness (*sgyu ma*). These are clearly based on Wuzhu's phrases, as reported in Pelliot tibétain 116 (see chapter 2). The commentary also ties the direct experience of the mind as nonexistent to the practice of the "single-method concentration" (*ting nge 'dzin tshul cig*), which is linked to the teachings of the patriarch Daoxin in the *Masters of the Laṅka* (see chapter 4).

The author of the commentary in Pelliot tibétain 699 is particularly fond of metaphors. The mind is like a stack of paper, with the pages con-stantly being turned. It is like a waterfall. In meditation, it can be like a lamp that the wind cannot extinguish. And the six senses are described in an extended series of similes:

> The delusory body engages with tangible objects, like a little
> bird snapping up a seed. The delusory mind engages with phe-

nomena, like a hand waving a flag. Delusory eyes engage with objects, like a goose looking at its own tail. Delusory ears engage with sounds, like a deer approaching a mountain pass. The delusory nose engages with smells, like a spirit waiting for burnt offerings. The delusory tongue engages with tastes, like drinking poisoned beer.

Some of these similes, like the deer approaching the mountain pass, the spirit waiting for burnt offerings, and drinking poisoned beer have a Tibetan flavor and suggest that this text and the sādhanas written in the same hand come from a Tibetan cultural milieu, more so than many of the other Zen texts that we have looked at in previous chapters. Another of the Zen manuscripts by this scribe, Pelliot tibétain 808, was also clearly composed in Tibet, as the way the author explains the terms "jewel" and "buddha" is entirely based on forms of the Tibetan words *dkon mchog* and *sangs rgyas*. So it seems that the scribe who wrote these manuscripts in the tenth century was copying texts that had been composed in the Tibetan language, perhaps in the Tibetan-speaking areas near Dunhuang after the fall of the Tibetan empire.

The sense that the author and audience of the commentary in Pelliot tibétain 699 lived in a culture familiar with both Zen and tantric practices is strengthened by the use of a mahāyoga text to justify a bit of Zen doctrine. To support the statement that the "unshakable concentration" mentioned in the root text is not merely an intellectual understanding of nonself, the author quotes the mahāyoga treatise *Questions and Answers on Vajrasattva,* which was popular enough at Dunhuang that it still exists in three different manuscript copies, one copied by hand by a high Chinese official. This gives some sense of the multicultural and multilingual scene in which Zen and mahāyoga practices flourished together.[9]

TEACHERS OF ZEN AND TANTRA

Is there anything else we can say about the Tibetan (or at least Tibetan-speaking) community that produced these manuscripts for tantric practice combined with Zen? At the end of the commentary in Pelliot tibétain 699, the scribe has added a few lines describing the nature of a master who teaches the sūtras and a master who teaches atiyoga. The latter is a synonym for "the great perfection" (*rdzogs chen*), a Tibetan practice tradition and literary genre that is found in a few Dunhuang manuscripts. At the time of the Dunhuang texts, that is, up to the end of the tenth century, the great perfection was primarily a way of practicing tantric sādhanas. One example of this can be seen in another manuscript by the same scribe as Pelliot tibétain 699, which has a poem on tantric practice:

> The teaching of the primordial, spontaneously present great
>   perfection,
> This sublime experiential domain of supreme insight
> Is bestowed as a precept upon those with intelligence;
> I pay homage to the definitive counsel spoken thus.
>
> Without center or periphery, neither one nor many,
> The maṇḍala that transcends thought and cannot be expressed
> Illuminates the mind of intrinsic awareness, wisdom, and knowledge;
> I pay homage to the great Vajrasattva.

These lines (and the further eight lines that follow in the manuscript) show that the great perfection was considered to be fully a part of the sādhana practices of mahāyoga. And they are strikingly similar in tone to the verses attributed to Namkai Nyingpo discussed in the previous chapter. It looks like Zen and atiyoga were performing similar functions at this time, providing the contemplative context to tantric sādhana practice. That is perhaps why the scribe in Pelliot tibétain 699 appended these lines on the two types of teacher. The two teachers offer parallel approaches to tantric practice.

Because of the way these lines have been laid out on the page, it is not entirely clear which description refers to which master.[10] The first question and answer can be reconstructed in this way:

> What is a master who teaches atiyoga like? A great garuda who
> cuts through the sky yet is aware of all living beings, clarifying
> the vehicles individually, yet cutting through space. "Clarifying"

means that he teaches the great meaning without mixing anything up. Like the sky-soaring garuda, he draws forth the greatness of the meaning, while teaching the divisions of the paths
that one should traverse.

This certainly ties in with the texts of atiyoga, in which the garuda
(Tib. *khyung*) features as a symbol and metaphor. The passage implies
that the teacher of atiyoga teaches the inner essence (or "meaning") of a
practice, without compromising or mixing up the details of the different
practices. This fits with the role of atiyoga/the great perfection as we see
it in other manuscripts. As for the teacher of sūtras, he or she is compared to another mythical bird, the king of the wild geese (Tib. *ngang
pa'i rgyal po,* Skt. *haṃsarāja*). In a story of the Buddha's previous lives, the
Haṃsa-jātaka, the king of the wild geese does not flee when freed from
a trap, but goes to the palace to teach the dharma to the king and queen.

What is a master who teaches the sūtras like? Like the king of
the geese who never hurries, he teaches the meaning of the lineage of masters, showing directly the practical application of
the words. He teaches the inappropriate to be appropriate for
those inferior scholars who are like young sheep climbing a rock
face, so that faults themselves are good qualities. Among many
people, he teaches the dharma with profound and meaningful
discourses that illuminate the depths. He teaches with a mind
that is like a hidden tortoise. Understanding the hidden secret is
the quality of such a master.

The teaching activity of this kind of master is that of a Zen teacher of
the instantaneous approach; it is the inferior scholars who climb slowly,
like young goats. The Zen context is also suggested by the phrase "the
lineage of masters," apparently an allusion to the patriarchs described in
texts like the *Masters of the Laṅka* and the narratives of Pelliot tibétain
996. This sūtra master's teaching is also described in terms of secrecy,
which as we have seen was invoked as much for Zen as it was for tantric
practices (see, for example, Guṇabhadra's description of his teachings in
the *Masters of the Laṅka*).

The way the scribe of Pelliot tibétain 699 has placed these two descriptions of teachers in apposition to each other does not suggest a comparison in which one must be superior to the other, or a hierarchy like that of the *Lamp for the Eyes of Contemplation*.[11] Rather it implies that the roles of the two types of teachers are complementary. They might be roles assumed by a single teacher, depending on the audience, just as a single scribe wrote both the tantric sādhanas in Pelliot tibétain 626 and 634 and the commentary on a Zen meditation in Pelliot tibétain 699. This kind of situation, rather than the sharp doctrinal distinctions set out in the *Lamp*, offers a better possibility of reconstructing how people put these texts into practice.

The Brief Precepts

All sentient beings, infinite in number, are in the prison of saṃsāra, the river of suffering, and the trap of ignorance. In order to destroy this and bring them to nirvāṇa with no aggregates remaining, do the following:

Cross your feet and hands. Straighten your back. Don't move your body. Don't say anything. Turn away without engaging the delusory six gates of the mind with their objects, and then look at your own mind. When you do, there is no substantiality to mind at all. So do not think of anything. Without engaging in the various emotional states, do not conceptualize anything. Once you have completely purified the mental sphere in this way, do not abide anywhere. Once you have sat for a long time, the mind will stabilize.

Suffering itself is enlightenment. Saṃsāra itself is nirvāṇa. The nature of wisdom does not arise at the beginning. It does not cease at the end, or abide in the present. The three times are empty in their equality. Emptiness itself is empty, so do not conceptualize emptiness as emptiness.

Once whatever arises is pacified, you need not deliberately obstruct and insistently suppress the mind and its basis endowed with coarse and subtle imprints. Since wisdom without apprehension and concentration without movement are one and the same, you will be gradually purified and forcefully self-liberated, not conceptualizing that which arises or abiding in the lack of arising.

In three sessions each day and night, cut out the heart of effort. Cultivate, without thinking, the wisdom that transcends thought. The scriptures say that thinking is not thinking, so do not even think about not having thoughts. Do not think "stop thinking!"[12]

The scriptures also say that this becomes more and more subtle, more and more clear, more and more equal. In the space of nonconceptualization, nonself shines forth. This dharma was entrusted to the great Kaśyapa. Dharmatāra meditated in this way. Nonconceptualization is clarity, and clarity is nonconceptual. This is the wisdom of your own awareness.

Nothing said here is an assertion.

The Commentary

Cross your feet and hands. Straighten your back. Don't move your body. Don't say anything.[13]

Applying the five mūdras, cultivate nonconceptualization. The mūdras are (i) settling the eyes on the nose, (ii) pressing the tongue to the roof of the mouth, (iii) placing the right hand on the left, (iv) placing the right foot on the left, (v) keeping the back straight. Settling the eyes on the nose eliminates the objects of vision. Pressing the tongue to the roof of the mouth eliminates the objects of speech and thought. Placing the right hand on the left eliminates the objects of apprehender and apprehended. Placing the right foot on the left eliminates the objects of coming and going. Bringing these together, you cultivate nonconceptualization.

Turn away without engaging the delusory six gates of the mind with their objects.

The delusory body engages with tangible objects, like a little bird snapping up a seed. The delusory mind engages with phenomena, like a hand waving a flag. Delusory eyes engage with objects, like a goose looking at its own tail. Delusory ears engage with sounds, like a deer approaching a mountain pass. The delusory nose engages with smells, like a spirit waiting for burnt offerings. The delusory tongue engages with tastes, like drinking poisoned beer.

The scriptures say: "Know that the six objects are deceptive, and consciousness is distracted in the hubbub; turn away without engaging with them." So, when a sage transforms the confused mind through the path of conceptual analysis, is that the mind's nirvāṇa? No, it is not like this.

The scriptures say: "The essential point of realization is nothing more than your own awareness."[14]

> *Look at your own mind. When you do, there is no substantiality*
> *to mind at all.*

When looking at your own mind, the method is this: there are eight questions about mind and where it abides. These eight questions about the mind are to be used deductively to come to a conclusion. Is the mind an apprehended object? Is it permanent? Is it transitory? Is it created? Is it terminated? Does it have the four colors? Does it have the eight shapes? Is it a knower?

It cannot be an apprehended object, because it engages with all kinds of objects. It is neither an apprehended object nor an apprehending subject either. Are the individual features of the mind each distinct objects? They are not, so it cannot be an apprehending subject of a multitude of objects either.

As for the claim that there is a permanent mind, it cannot be permanent, because even in the mere snap of a finger, the eyes of the hearers can count 360 moments. It is like when you have 360 sheets of paper that you need to pierce, you count each one as you pierce it—the continuum of mind is just like that. As for the claim that it is transitory, this is also not the case. Since it is possible to engage intently with an external object like a butter lamp unmoved by the wind, mind cannot be transitory.

"Well then, this mind must be created." It is not created either. It is not established as an entity, a feature, a shape. It is not created, or terminated. Mind is like a waterfall: it moves, wavers, and engages with all objective aspects. Thus mind is not terminated.

"Well, then is mind uncreated?" The profound and unique activity is to meditate and analyze with the dynamic energy of insight. When a sage analyzes, does he look for something other, or not? In the scriptures it says:

> The meaning of understanding how things are is no more than
> one's own awareness. That awareness is like this: it cannot be giv-
> en a name or expressed. This meaning cannot be denied. There

is not even an atom of an experience of the mind. To have what is known as "experience and awareness of something other" is to fall to the level of the hearers and solitary buddhas.

> *Without engaging in the various emotional states, do not conceptualize anything.*

Now you should practice the three precepts, three instructions, and three seed syllables (OM, AH, HUM). Since the mind has no essence whatsoever, *do not think of anything* and practice nonthought. Not thinking about the essence of mind, *do not conceptualize emotional states in any way* and practice nonconceptualization. Because mind does not abide anywhere, practice nonabiding.

Now practice the three instructions. Mind is not established anywhere, so practice nonmind. Mind is not an object of recollection, so practice nonrecollection. There are no objects to recollect, so practice illusoriness.

Also, when the mind has no essence whatsoever, this is the practice of morality. When you do not mentally engage with the afflictions, this is the practice of concentration. When mental experiences are purified in this way, "not abiding anywhere" is the practice of insight. When you pour water into an unbroken vessel, the reflections of the sun and moon appear there. Just so, when you cultivate a single-pointed concentration, once this concentration is achieved, the insight of vipaśyanā is born in you. The above shows the method for settling the mind.

> *Once you have completely purified the mental sphere in this way, after a long time the mind will become stable.*

The scriptures say that mind is like lightning, wind, and rain. It is like the waves of a great lake. As long as the nonconceptual mind has not been experienced, the nature of meditation is like the activity of a fighter. Thus one should constantly discipline joy and excitement. When mind transforms into a state of insubstantiality and nonconceptualization, it is disciplined and unwavering. This is how one's mind should be constantly disciplined.

> *Uncreated and unarising, suffering itself is enlightenment.*
> *Saṃsāra itself is nirvāṇa. The nature of wisdom does not*
> *arise at the beginning.*

Though not associated with suffering, enlightenment is not separate from it either. Phenomena have always been without self; they are un-arisen from the beginning. When one realizes the nature of reality, one knows it through insight, and the meaning of the state of reality is realized without error.

> *It does not cease at the end, or abide in the present.*

Once the unceasing mind has been realized, you should not abide in the present. The meaning of this is not to apply the label "this is it." And one should not apply this meaning as a label either.

> *The three times are empty in their equality.*

This is not the complete emptiness of the three times, but emptiness as the equality of the three times.

> *Emptiness itself is empty,*

Reality itself is empty in its emptiness.

> *So do not conceptualize emptiness as emptiness.*

Something that is empty is not this kind of emptiness. Thus when we say "empty," this does not mean establishing that something is simply empty.

> *Once whatever arises is pacified in awareness,*

Awareness is not experienced as pleasant or unpleasant. The arisings are like thieves; awareness is like a sentinel. External awareness is the mind projecting the five sensual qualities.

You need not deliberately obstruct and insistently suppress
the mind and its basis endowed with eighty-four kinds of
imprints.

When you internalize the antidote to the hearers' pacification, even movement is equalized as the basic syllable A. There is no need for anything except to cultivate equilibrium through śamatha without the method of śamatha and vipaśyanā without the method of vipaśyanā.

Gradually purified and forcefully self-liberated,

Within the equilibrium of śamatha and vipaśyanā, immediately practice the vajra-like samadhi on the ground of buddhahood known as "universal light."

Not apprehending insight,

Not apprehending insight means cultivating nonconceptual śamatha three times a day and three times a night.

And equalizing the unshakable concentration,

The unshakable concentration is not merely seeing insight. "Equalizing" means that merely to see Mount Meru is not to climb it. Where is this shown? In *Questions and Answers on Vajrasattva*:

> Completely abandon this grasping at self;
> That which grasps phenomena has no independent self.[15]

This is what is to be seen. As for abiding, do not abide anywhere, not in external objects and not in the internal mind.

Not conceptualizing that which arises or abiding in the lack of
arising.

Do not conceptualize the six senses, but do not abide without vivid awareness or arisings either. And do not distinguish between coarse and subtle in your own mind. If you do not engage in the slightest bit of activity, there will be no chance of even a moment's distraction.

> *In three sessions each day and night, cut out the heart of effort.*

Cultivate nonconceptualization three times a day and three times a night.

> *Cultivate, without thinking, the wisdom that transcends thought.*

This is the conclusion of meditating in this way.

> *The scriptures say that thinking is not thinking, so do not even think about not having thoughts.*

There is no thinking about nonconceptualization, or about anything else.

> *The scriptures also say that one should not think "stop thinking!"*

Do not think in order to clarify the meaning of nonconceptuality.

> *This becomes more and more subtle, more and more peaceful, more and more clear, more and more equal.*

Once the basis has been transformed, rest in equanimity in the space of reality. Apply this up to the very subtlest aspects of the latent imprints of the basis. Purify and clarify the state of mind's wisdom.

> *This dharma was entrusted to the great Kaśyapa.*

It was entrusted to the lineage of twenty-eight Indian scholars, ending with Dharmatāra.

Dharmatāra meditated in this way.

He clarified nonself in persons and in phenomena.

> *Nonconceptualization is clarity, and clarity is nonconceptual.*
> *This is the wisdom of your own awareness. Nothing said*
> *here is an assertion.*

The end.

What is a master who teaches atiyoga like? A great garuda who cuts through the sky yet is aware of all living beings, clarifying the vehicles individually, yet cutting through space. "Clarifying" means that he teaches the great meaning without mixing anything up. Like the sky-soaring garuda, he draws forth the greatness of the meaning, while teaching the divisions of the paths that one should traverse.

What is a master who teaches the sūtras like? Like the king of the swans who never hurries, he teaches the meaning of the lineage of masters, showing directly the practical application of the words. He teaches the inappropriate to be appropriate for those inferior scholars who are like young sheep climbing a rock face, so that faults themselves are good qualities. Among many people, he teaches the dharma with profound and meaningful discourses that illuminate the depths. He teaches with a mind that is like a hidden tortoise. Understanding the hidden secret is the quality of such a master. Thus it is said.

Notes

Introduction

1. Though *Zen* is a Japanese word, in this book I use it as the general name for the family of traditions in Chinese, Tibetan, Japanese, Korean, and other languages. *Zen* is the Japanese pronunciation of the characters first used in China to transliterate the Sanskrit *dhyāna,* "meditation." It might be more accurate to refer to the Chinese traditions as *Chan* and the Korean as *Son,* while the Tibetans used their translation of the Sanskrit, *Samten* (*bsam brtan*). However, *Zen* is used here across these linguistic distinctions for the sake of simplicity. Note that there are also surviving Zen texts in the Turkic and Tangut languages; these have not yet been much studied, but see Zieme 2012 and Solonin 2000. On the other hand, the use of the single term *Zen* should not be taken to imply a single tradition unchanging across time and space.

2. Adamek 2011, 33. See also Adamek 2007 for a detailed discussion of the historical development of the precepts ceremony in China, with regard to Chan lineages.

3. The classic translation and study of the *Platform Sutra* is Yampolsky 1967. The classic analysis of the historical development of the text is Yanagida 1967. In the latter, Yanagida argues that the original core of the text comprises the bestowal of the "formless precepts" and subsequent meditation instructions (sections 20–30) along with the lineage (section 51). Yanagida argues that the author of this original text was a monk called Wuxing Fahai who lived in the eighth century. See the summary in English of Yanagida's study in McRae 1993. See also the study of the different versions of the *Platform Sutra* in the Dunhuang manuscripts in Anderl 2013. Anderl suggests that the original referent of the term "platform sūtra" was the *Vajracchedikā,* which was so called due to its central role in Zen ordination rituals. The platform sermon of Shenhui is translated in Liebenthal 1953. The Japanese catalogs of Saicho (767–822) and Ennin (793–864) also contain sequences of texts suggestive of these platform rituals, with the bodhisattva precepts followed by relevant sūtras and Zen texts (see Lin 2011, 42–53). The extended nature of the ceremony is discussed in Adamek 2007, 197–204 (which includes a passage by Zongmi on this subject). The *Record of the Dharma Jewel through the Generations* mentions a brief precepts retreat as lasting "only three days and three nights" (Adamek 2007, 348).

4. The study of the oral background to texts in the Pali canon is quite advanced, both in terms of their oral origins and their use as sources for sermons in later traditions. See Langer 2013 for an overview of these discussions and a study of the practice of sermons

in Sri Lankan Buddhist traditions. Along with the many catechisms written in Christian cultures, one could also compare the *Pandects of Holy Scripture* by Antiochus of Palestine and the paraphrases of Erasmus in their use as sourcebooks for sermons.

5. Such marks in texts used for lectures or liturgies are quite common in the Chinese manuscripts from Dunhuang (see Mair 1981) but have not previously been noted among the Tibetan manuscripts. Anderl (2013, 169) has discussed the presence of "performance markers" in manuscripts of the *Platform Sutra*. A further use of the *Platform Sutra* is mentioned by Barrett (2005, 116): the possession of the physical manuscript was accepted as proof of membership in a Zen lineage.

6. Wright 2008, 4.

7. For a survey of the meanings of "ritual," see the introduction to Lin 2011.

8. McRae 2003, 11–21. In the current section on Chinese Zen, or Chan, I use the latter term as this is the general practice of McRae and others who are quoted extensively here.

9. Ibid., 19.

10. In the *Treatise on the Essentials of Cultivating the Mind* attributed to Hongren (601–774) but probably composed by his students.

11. Shenhui's own characterization of his position as the "Southern School" of Chan while those of Shenxiu's students' being the "Northern School" was part of his self-positioning, and despite being used by some recent scholars as if it represented actual historical schools, this distinction should be treated with care. On Wuzhu and Sichuan Chan, see Adamek 2007.

12. McRae 2003, 56–60.

13. See van Schaik and Iwao 2008.

14. This is the suggestion in Bretfeld 2004.

15. See Jackson 1994.

16. Demiéville 1952.

17. The *Zen Book* (*Bsam gtan gi yi ge*) is listed in the *Ldan dkar ma* (Lalou 1953, 333–34). Other Zen texts in the *Ldan dkar ma* and *'Phang thang ma* are discussed in Faber 1985, 49–50.

18. See Kapstein (2000, 75–78) for elements of Zen in the teachings of Gampopa and his students and Stearns (1996, 149n78) for a discussion of the Zen teachings of Künpang and the comments of Tāranātha on the *Mdo sde brgyad bcu khungs*. Tāranātha assumed that this text was the work of Moheyan, part of a general trend in Tibet, as Zen influence declined, to attribute all Zen texts to the only Zen master who remained well known in Tibet. See also Meinert 2006.

19. Sørensen 1989, 135.

20. Much work on this material has been done by Victor Mair (see, for example, Mair 1981, 1983). For a summary of Chinese popular literature from Dunhuang, see Schmid 2001.

21. Ueyama 1982, 88–121.

22. A rare reference to a Zen temple is found in the colophon to Pelliot chinois 2292, dated to the year 947; however, the temple mentioned is in Sichuan (see Mair 1981, 11). There are a few examples of monks identifying themselves as "Chan monks," such as in Pelliot chinois 3051.

23. The most complete catalog of Chinese Zen manuscripts is Yanagida 1974. The most complete catalog of the Tibetan Zen manuscripts is van Schaik 2014.

24. A similar list oriented more to the Chinese manuscripts is given in Sørensen 1989, 118–20.

25. Another useful set of manuscripts for understanding the practical and ritual nature of Zen is the one containing a text known as *The Twelve Hours of Meditation* (see Jao and Demiéville 1971).

26. See van Schaik 2013.

27. Elsewhere I suggested that manuscripts like this show signs of being written down from oral sources; see van Schaik 2007.

28. Jones 2004, 335.

29. The concept of affordances was developed by James Gibson (1979). Later Donald Norman (1988) developed a "psychology of everyday things" based on the concept of affordance, applying it specifically to the designed features of human-made objects such as doors. The affordance concept has been given a wider historical and cultural application by Tim Ingold (2000).

CHAPTER 1: ORIENTATIONS

1. For a detailed discussion of Pelliot tibétain 116 and its texts, see van Schaik 2014, 50–57.

2. The *Lamp for the Eyes of Contemplation* (Gnubs sangs rgyas ye shes 1974, 57) presents these two stages—generating the awakening mind and then immediately moving to the nonconceptual—as the fundamental method of the instantaneous approach.

3. Kimura (1980) correctly identified this as a single textual unit under the title given explicitly on v47.2. An English translation, with identifications of the scriptural citations, can be found in Faber 1985. See also the discussion of the citations from masters of meditation in Meinert 2007b, 190–92.

4. The *Mi rtog pa'i bsgom don* is found in the *Bstan 'gyur* (D.3910). Another similar question and answer text is represented in Pelliot tibétain 821, which is almost complete, and the fragments IOL Tib J 706 and Pelliot tibétain 817 (which are both from the same original manuscript). Some sūtra quotes (not the questions and answers) are also found verbatim in the *Lamp for the Eyes of Contemplation* and the *Mdo sde brgyad bcu khungs* (IOL Tib J 705 and Pelliot tibétain 818).

5. There is an interesting discussion of intertextuality in the Buddhist and Bonpo *Phurpa* tantras in Cantwell and Mayer 2013. Based on the schema of the Hebraist Peter Schäfer, the authors discuss the idea of three levels of text, *lemmata, microform,* and *macroform*.

6. See, for example, the work on eighteenth-century British miscellanies in the Digital Miscellanies Index, www.digitalmiscellaniesindex.org.

7. On the question and answer format among Chinese Chan texts and its Chinese antecedents, see McRae 2003. Compare the *Questions and Answers on Vajrasattva*, an important question and answer text written for Tibetan practitioners of tantric mahāyoga, a complex of practices that was also being introduced to Tibet through rituals of initiation (Takahashi 2010).

8. Surprisingly, no previous study of Pelliot tibétain 116 took any account of this note. The lacuna in this part of Pelliot tibétain 116 was noted by Ryūtoku Kimura (1976), but he did not consult the interlinear note, or the notes on VI, and therefore slightly misplaced the point at which the lacuna occurs.

9. The text in Pelliot tibétain 116 breaks off here, and the answer to this question is incomplete. The following question is taken from *Mi rtog pa'i bsgom don*, f.12b, before we turn to the copy of the *Single Method* in Pelliot tibétain 823.

10. From this point the text is taken from Pelliot tibétain 823; the sūtra title is missing, but the same quote appears in the *Mi rtog pa'i bsgom don*, f.12b.

11. The text resumes on the verso of Pelliot tibétain 116 at this point.

12. There is an ellipsis in the Pelliot tibétain 116 version, and in the Pelliot tibétain 21 version as well. My translation here has been slightly corrected based on the canonical version.

CHAPTER 2: MASTERS OF MEDITATION

1. McRae 2003, xix, 5–6.

2. Austin [1962] 1971, esp. lecture 8. Austin distinguishes between *illocutionary* and *perlocutionary* features of speech, the first being the performative features of what is said, and the second being the consequences of saying something; as Austin ([1962] 1971, 110) points out, statements that in themselves do not appear to be actions may cause important consequences: "for you may convince me that she is an adultress by asking her whether it was not her handkerchief that was in X's bedroom, or by stating that it was hers." In this sense, the performative features of most of the texts in Pelliot tibétain 116 and other manuscripts are perlocutionary in that they are not explicit statements of, for example, taking a vow (the exception in Pelliot tibétain 116 is the *Prayer of Excellent Conduct*).

3. Searle 1976, 3. The example Searle uses, taken from Elizabeth Anscombe, is of a man going around a town with a shopping list, being followed by a detective who is writing down everything he buys; the two lists may end up exactly the same, but their function is completely different: the first is performative, the second descriptive.

4. Latour 2005.

5. In *Structuralist Poetics,* the classic work of structuralist literary criticism, Jonathan Culler (1975) argues that public systems of conventions allow readers to respond to texts, that these are quite different in different textual genres, and that these conventions are implicit in the structural features of the texts.

6. McRae 2003, 58. McRae's example is the *Treatise on the Transcendence of Cognition (Juegan lun).*

7. The concept of "emotional energy" as the effect of a successful group ritual has been elaborated by Randall Collins (2004, 102–33).

8. The Chinese manuscripts containing collected teachings of Zen masters are BD01199, Or.8210/S.2715, and Pelliot chinois 2923 and 4795. See Broughton 1999 for a translation of the Chinese text and correspondences to the Tibetan translations in the *Lamp for the Eyes of Contemplation.*

CHAPTER 3: TEACHERS AND STUDENTS

1. Zongmi, *Chan Prolegomenon* (*Chanyuan zhuquanji duxu*), section 19, translated in Broughton 2009, 118–19.
2. See Faure 1997, 178–80; McRae 2003, 56–60.
3. IOL Tib J 704 contains what may be a commentary on this text. Since various passages are commented upon that do not appear here in IOL Tib J 710, the current text may be incomplete. The original is probably a translation from a Chinese text. As such, the subject matter seems to be unusual; according to John McRae (2003, 91), "as with all Chan literature at this time (not to mention the texts of other schools), the aspiring student is still invisible."
4. Tibetan, D.107, 93b–94a; Sanskrit, Nanjio, pp. 97–98; Chinese, T.672, 602a. The original Sanskrit term is *tathāgataṃ dhyāna*. The Tibetan translation is *de bzhin gshegs pa'i bsam gtan* and the Chinese is *rulai chan*.
5. Adamek 2007, 339–340.
6. See for example Eastman 1983, 58.
7. Tibetan, D.107, 55a; Sanskrit, Nanjio 1923, 10; Chinese, T.672, 588c. The Sanskrit is *mahāyogayogino;* the Tibetan is *rnal 'byor chen po'i rnal 'byor can,* and the Chinese is *daxiuxing wei xiuxingshi* ("the great yoga" being *daxiuxing*). In Japanese Zen, the same term (*daishugyō*) appears as the subject of the sixty-eighth section of the *Shōbōgenzō* collection.
8. This doctor simile is also used in the same context in IOL Tib J 709 (text 5), 23r.
9. The first part of this sentence has been inserted as an interlinear note.
10. See Pelliot tibétain 699, translated in chapter 10, which explains the eight aspects of contemplating the mind.
11. A part of this passage (9r.1–3) is quoted in IOL Tib J 704 (r2.4–r3.4); while marked as a citation in the latter, no text name is given there.

CHAPTER 4: THE PRACTICE OF GENEALOGY

1. The full title of the text is *Record of the Masters and Students of the Laṅka* (*Lenqie shizi ji* in Chinese, *Ling ka'i mkhan po dang slob ma'i mdo* in Tibetan), where "Laṅka" refers to the lineage of transmission of the *Laṅkāvatāra sūtra*.
2. See Kieschnick 1997 and Shinohara 1998, 306–7. In particular, Daoxuan's *Further Biographies of Eminent Monks* is a major source for the *Masters of the Laṅka*.
3. All of these lineage accounts are preserved in the Taisho version of the Chinese Buddhist canon. *Record of the Dharma Jewel through the Generations* (*Lidai fabao ji*) is T.2075; *Record of the Masters and Students of the Laṅka* (*Lenqie shizi ji*) is T.2837; *Record of the Transmission of the Dharma Jewel* (*Chuan fabao ji*) is T.2075; and *Record of the Transmission of the Lamp* (*Jingde chuandeng lu*) is T.2076.
4. Shinohara 1998, 306.
5. See Lin 2011, chap. 2, and Faure 1997, chap. 6.
6. Adamek 2007, 164–65.

7. Faure 1997, 156–57; Jao and Demiéville 1971, 87.

8. McRae 2003, 8.

9. The Chinese text is extant in the canon (T.85, n.2837) and several Dunhuang manuscripts. Pelliot chinois 3436 is nearly complete but lacking the preface by Jingjue (683–750?). The long scroll Or.8210/S.2054 has the preface, but the text breaks off in the middle of the section on the teacher Daoxin. Further fragments are found in Pelliot chinois 3294, 3537, 3703, and 4564, and Or.8210/S.4272. Drikung Kyabgön Chetsang (2010) has published an edition of the *Masters of the Laṅka* including a translation of the second part of the Chinese text into Tibetan.

10. On authorship in European manuscript cultures, see Dagenais 1994. See also Cabezón 2001 for an inquiry into authorship in Tibet.

11. Here I am following the suggestions of Ueyama (1971) rather than Stein (1983) and Faure (1997, 170–71). There is truth in Stein's idea of a Chinese translation vocabulary in Tibetan; for example, we see in the *Masters of the Laṅka* that some Tibetan words used to translate Chinese terms have a different meaning from their use when seen in other translated texts; examples include *gzhung* for the Chinese *li* ("principle") and *phyi mo* for *ben* ("fundamental").

12. The single practice concentration is *gcig spyod pa'i ting nge 'dzin* in Tibetan, translating the Chinese *yixing sanmei*, which in turn was used to translate the Sanskrit *ekavyūhasamādhi* (single magnificence concentration) and *ekākārasamādhi* (single mode concentration). See Faure 1997, 67–69.

13. An earlier source records that Guṇabhadra arrived in China in the twelfth year of the Yuanjia period, that is, 435. See Glass 2007, 38.

14. Sūtra quotations in this text cannot easily be matched to the extant canonical literature and seem to have been translated directly from the Chinese without reference to the authorized Tibetan scriptural translations. This could be taken as further evidence that the *Masters of the Laṅka* is an early translation.

15. IOL Tib J 710 has "not virtue," but here I follow the Chinese text, as the Tibetan seems to be a scribal error.

16. The Chinese versions contain further text here with more sayings attributed to Guṇabhadra, of a different character.

17. Note the slightly different name for this practice here compared with the list above (*reg pa/'thun pa*).

18. The Chinese version of the *Masters of the Laṅka* has more text here, with further teachings attributed to Bodhidharma. These include the "questions about things" that McRae and others have suggested as early precedents for the encounter dialogue. Their absence here, as with the absent material in other masters' sections, suggests that these parts were later additions to the text, not present when it was translated into Tibetan (late eighth century?) but added by the time of the Chinese manuscripts (ninth to tenth centuries). This is the conclusion of Daishun Ueyama, reiterated by Faure (1997, 168–69).

19. In other sources Huike is always said to be from Wulao, Henan. Here the Tibetan *Stsang chu* is probably a slightly garbled transliteration of Songshan, the sacred mountain in Henan where the Shaolin Temple is located

20. This long quotation is actually a paraphrase of a verse passage from book 12 of the Chinese translation of the *Avataṃsaka*. The Chinese version of the *Masters of the Laṅka* gives this quote in an expanded version that is somewhat closer to the sūtra. However, unlike the previous sections, there is no other extra material in the Chinese version after this point.

21. The Tibetan here is *Hwang kong*. Cleary (1986, 44) has "Neishan Temple." On the stūpa and inscriptions dedicated to Sengcan at Huangong, see Adamek 1997, 473n131.

22. Since the Chinese text continues here without a break, it appears that the Tibetan here is only a translation of the first fascicle (*bam po*) of the Chinese text that was its basis. Yet the manuscript IOL Tib J 710 appears to be complete, so it seems that this Tibetan text was copied and preserved as a textual unit.

Chapter 5: Encounter and Emptiness

1. Translation from Ferguson 2011, 82.

2. For a definition of "encounter dialogue," see McRae 2003, 77–78.

3. Another text, a Tibetan translation of a Chinese original, features a question and answer dialogue between the master Zhida (a disciple of Shenxiu active in the early eighth century) and a student. This is the *Dunwu zhenzong yaojue*, which appears as the eighth text in Pelliot tibétain 116. A preface (not found in the Tibetan translation) states that the master and student here actually represent the mind of a single adept. The Tibetan text has been studied by Ueyama (1976) and, largely based on this, by Tanaka and Roberston (1992). Though this text clearly represents a form of literature that influenced the later encounter dialogues, it does not contain the provocative style of answers found here in *The Practice of the Instantaneous Approach*.

4. Translation from McRae 1986, 173, 180.

5. John McRae (2003) appears ambivalent about whether to view encounter dialogue as a literary form or as a record of an oral tradition's recording actual monastic encounters. Alan Cole (2009, 10–11) criticizes McRae for this, characterizing him, perhaps unfairly, as assuming that "it was the masters who made the tradition and not their clever historians."

6. See van Schaik (2007) on manuscripts written in rough hands that may be from oral sources, and van Schaik and Galambos (2012, 30–34) on manuscripts possibly written by non-Tibetans.

7. On the Chinese manuscripts written by lay students, see Mair 1981.

8. This version is the eighth text in IOL Tib J 709. Another version is found in IOL Tib J 706 and Pelliot tibétain 812. Other Madhyamaka texts among the Zen manuscripts include the *Prajñāśataka-nāma-prakaraṇa* of Nāgārjuna in IOL Tib J 617 and the excerpts from Nāgārjuna and Āryadeva in the *Single Method* in Pelliot tibétain 116.

9. van Schaik 2004a, 79–80.

10. *Distinguishing the Views* (*Lta ba'i khyad pa*) is found in Pelliot tibétain 814; the canonical version is D.4360. Other manuscripts with texts on the distinctions between different philosophical views include IOL Tib J 693 and Pelliot tibétain 842. The last of these

differs slightly from the names of the two divisions of the Madhyamaka, using "outer Madhyamaka" and "inner yogic Madhyamaka." See the brief discussion of some of these Dunhuang manuscripts and related canonical literature in Karmay [1988] 2007, 149–51.

11. There seems to be some corruption in the manuscript copy as there is no question marker, and the line *ci ltar na chos thams cad* is repeated

12. Vṛthāsuta is a reconstruction of a possible Sanskrit term behind the Tibetan transliteration *'bri ta spu ta*. It would mean something on the lines of "emerging randomly."

CHAPTER 6: DEBATE

1. The *Ratification* mentions that a queen from the Dro clan was a principal supporter of Moheyan. And in the lineage history in Pelliot tibétain 996 (see chapter 9), an eminent member of this clan is mentioned as a supporter of the master Pug Yeshe Yang. The Dro ('Bro) and Ba (Dba') clans seem to have been increasingly pitted against each other toward the end of the Tibetan empire and in the era following its fall. This rivalry has been put forward as the background to the assassination of the emperor Relpachen in the late 830s (see Yamaguchi 1996). After the empire began to fall apart, the first major civil war was at the northern borders, where a governor of the Dro clan allied himself with the new Chinese rulers, while a general from the Ba clan fought to establish himself as a local warlord (see Petech 1994).

2. Translated from Demiéville [1952] 2006, 39–41.

3. Translated from ibid., 42.

4. On suspicions about the veracity of the account of the Huatai debate, see Jørgensen 2005, 64–65. On the wide influence of this debate story, see Yanagida 1983.

5. For a translation of the *Testimony of Ba* version, see Pasang and Diemberger 2000. The Tibetan narrative of the debate at Samye has been discussed in numerous papers; see, for example, Imaeda 1975 and Seyfort Ruegg 1992. On the negative and positive responses to the figure of Moheyan in Tibet over the centuries, see van Schaik 2003.

6. The passage from the *Lamp for the Eyes of Contemplation* is Gnubs sangs rgyas ye shes 1974, 15.1–5. The text is not at all clear, and the translation in Karmay [1988] 2007, 92–95 should be considered provisional. The three texts attributed to Kamalaśīla, all with the name *The Stages of Meditation,* are found in D.3915–17: *Bsgom pa'i rim pa,* Skt. *Bhāvanākrama.* On the thematic connections between this text and the *Ratification,* see Gómez 1983b.

7. On later attempts at a historical reconstruction using the *Ratification* and the *Testimony,* see Yampolsky 1983.

8. See the texts translated in McRae 1986.

9. Poceski 2008, 87.

10. Also missing in the Tibetan text is a quotation from the sūtra *The Crown Prominence of the Buddha* (Chinese original: T.953). On the reconstruction of the Tibetan text, see van Schaik 2014, 37–39.

11. *Pace* Gómez 1983a, in this text *gzhung* usually refers to scriptures, not to the "universal principle" (Ch. *li*) as in the *Masters of the Laṅka.*

12. This first section of the text, up to and including question 3, is taken from Pelliot tibétain 827.

13. This phrase is not found in the *Vajracchedikā,* though it does appear in several other sūtras. In general, the citations of textual authority here seem to be references to the general positions of the sūtras, rather than direct quotations.

14. From this question onward, the text is taken from Pelliot tibétain 823.

15. This question and the remainder of the text are not in the Chinese version.

16. The remainder of the extant text—the last line on Pelliot tibétain 823 recto and the whole of IOL Tib J 703 recto—is directly taken from the *Avataṃsaka* (D.44, 207b–208a). This passage is a set of ten verses spoken by the bodhisattva Dharmaśrī to the bodhisattva Mañjuśrī.

17. Here a verse is skipped that is found in the canonical and *Sūtrasamuccaya* versions.

18. Only part of the first line of this verse is extant, but the rest is likely to have followed. This is the last verse of this verse section of the *Avataṃsaka.*

Chapter 7: Observing the Mind

1. On the teachers of Moheyan, see Demiéville [1952] 2006, 125n6 and Demiéville 1973, 345–46. In the latter work, Demiéville states that the figures said to be Moheyan's teachers are associated with the Northern School and notes that the Southern School is never mentioned in the *Ratification.*

2. For Moheyan's position as Shenhui's student in Zongmi's lineage chart, see Broughton 2009, 79. For an argument against this possibility on doctrinal grounds, see Faure 1997, 128–29, 219n82. More recently, John Jørgensen (2005, 596) has simply stated that Moheyan was a pupil of Shenhui, who "tried to harmonize 'Northern Ch'an' . . . with the Southern Ch'an of Shen-hui and the Platform Sutra." This seems quite in line with the general trend in the generation after Shenhui to bridge the doctrinal gap between sudden and gradual that he had opened up.

3. See Faure 1997, 178–80; McRae 2003, 56–60.

4. O rgyan gling pa 1983, 570. The passage in the *Lamp for the Eyes of Contemplation* is Gnubs sangs rgyas ye shes 1974, 15. For the text and translation, see Tucci [1958] 1978, 378–79, 391–93. See also the discussion in Karmay [1988] 2007, 90–96. Karmay shows how this text reworks the parallel passage in the *Lamp for the Eyes of Contemplation.*

5. Demiéville [1952] 2006, 25. In a note on this sentence, Demiéville suggests that the author is referring to esoteric initiations: "le sens est plûtot qu'il s'agissait d'initiations ésotériques, et non de prédications publiques."

6. John McRae (2005) has discussed the ordination platform movement in this period; see McRae (2005, 86 and 91–92) for a discussion of the esoteric aspect of Yixing's platform. The abbreviated title of the Dunhuang text is *Ritual Guidelines for the Platform Dharma* (*Tanfa yize*). The most complete manuscript is Pelliot chinois 3913; this was copied by Yuanshou, who also copied a number of other tantric manuscripts, including Pelliot chinois 3835, which is dated 978. Other manuscripts with parts of this text include Pelliot chinois 2791, 3213; Or.8210/S.2316, 5981. This text has been studied by Tanaka Ryōshū (1981).

7. As Carmen Meinert (2006) has shown, all Zen texts known (if only by their title) in Tibet came to be attributed to Moheyan.

8. *Kun mkhyen zhal lung*, 527–28, quoted in van Schaik 2003.

9. *Testimony of Ba,* 20v.

10. The final line is found only in *Lamp for the Eyes of Contemplation* (Gnubs sangs rgyas ye shes 1974, 165.4–5).

11. The Chinese canonical version is T.953; the Tibetan canonical version is D.236. This sūtra is discussed at length in Demiéville 2007, 43–52, referred to there by the Sanskrit title *Śūraṃgama sūtra*. The sūtra is also quoted in the *Single Method* (see chapter 1).

12. On the practice of "observing the mind" in the work of Shenxiu, see McRae 1986, 196–218; Faure 1997, 58–67. Wolun's text is found in Or.8210/S.1494 and S.6103. The passage on observing the mind in *Mahā-uṣṇīṣa sūtra* is at D.236, 277b–278a.

13. Gómez 1983a, 98.

14. A distinction of three types of students was famously used by Atisha in his *Lamp for the Path to Enlightenment* in the eleventh century and was important in the Tibetan Dzogchen exegetical tradition: see van Schaik 2004a, 115–24.

15. Two passages from a *Meditation Precepts* (*Bsgom lung*) of Moheyan are quoted in *Lamp for the Eyes of Contemplation* (Gnubs sangs rgyas ye shes 1974, 145–46). The first occurs in IOL Tib J 468, the second in IOL Tib J 709.

16. The same passage appears in *Lamp for the Eyes of Contemplation* (Gnubs sangs rgyas ye shes 1974, 145.5–146.3).

17. A similar passage appears in *Lamp for the Eyes of Contemplation* (Gnubs sangs rgyas ye shes 1974, 146.3–5).

18. This quotation matches a verse from the *Guhyasamāja tantra,* apart from one line. The verse is found at D.442, 95a.

CHAPTER 8: AUTHORITY AND PATRONAGE

1. Pasang and Diemberger 2000, 47–52 (ff.8b–10b). This is the *Dba' bzhed,* the earliest extant version of the *Testimony of Ba.* In this version, the trip to China occurs not in the emperor's childhood but later in the narrative, after Śāntarakṣita's first visit to Tibet. But this seems to be a mistake, as Ba Sangshi refers to the emperor's being too young to study Buddhism, and Kim makes a prophecy referring to the future time when the emperor reaches adulthood. In other versions of the text, the journey and the meeting with the Reverend Kim do occur earlier in the narrative, during the childhood of Tri Song Detsen.

2. For Zongmi's account of Kim, see Broughton 1983, 30–38; and 2009, 232n160. On Kim in the *Record,* see Adamek 2007, 275–76, 337–38.

3. See Adamek 2007, 206, 246, 338 and Broughton 2009, 183.

4. Pelliot tibétain 116, f.174r.

5. The same presentation appears in the Tibetan works *Lamp for the Eyes of Contemplation* and *The Ministers' Edict.* These correspondences have been noted in Faber 1985, 73n104.

6. This text, titled *Excerpt from the Seven Lineage Masters' Principles of Meditation* (*Mkhan po bdun rgyud kyi bsam brtan gyi mdo las 'byung ba*), appears in Pelliot tibétain 813,

f.4v. Some Tibetan translations of Chinese apocryphal sūtras have been linked with the Baotang lineage, due to the role these sūtras play in the *Record*. See Obata 1974 (and also Ueyama 1983, 332–33). However, the use of these sūtras was not exclusive to the Baotang lineage.

7. On Tankuang and his treatise, see Pachow 1979a, 1979b and Ueyama 1990, chap. 1. The four manuscripts used by Pachow for his study are Pelliot tibétain 2077 and 2576, and Or.8210/S.2720 and 2732. The translation here is from Pachow 1979b, 35.

8. Translation from Meinert 2007a, 250.

9. On the various theories of the date of the Tibetan conquest of Dunhuang, see Ueyama 1990, 25–32 and Iwao 2011.

10. Ueyama's work on Chödrup/Facheng, collected in Ueyama 1990, chap. 2, is the most detailed and extensive study available.

11. IOL Tib J 219, f.144r.

12. Ueyama 1990, 112–16. One further panel from this manuscript is found in Pelliot tibétain 609. Ueyama suggests that Chödrup first translated the whole of the commentary and then extracted the root text for his translation of the sūtra. A similarly annotated Chinese copy of the *Yogacaryābhūmiśāstra* (Pelliot tibétain 783) may also be from Chödrup.

13. The version of the Maudgalyāyana story (IOL Tib J 633) has been discussed in depth in Kapstein 2007. The text on Madhyamaka is found in IOL Tib J 1772 and 1773. The bilingual (Sino-Tibetan) text in IOL Tib J 683 has been transcribed, translated, and discussed in Thomas, Miyamoto, and Clauson 1929.

14. R. A. Stein (1983, 154–56) discussed this text briefly. Stein (1984) also analyzed in detail the manuscript on the seals, IOL Tib J 506. See also the English translations of these articles in Stein 2010. The manuscript in question, IOL Tib J 709, has also been studied by Ryūtoku Kimura (1976, 1980, 1981). Kimura (1981, 127) argues that the *Chan Document* does not appear to be a translation from Chinese, based on the vocabulary therein. However, the grammar suggests neither a translation from an Indic source nor an indigenous literary production. Stein (1983, 155–56) suggests that the text contains a mixture of the vocabulary used to translate Indic and Chinese texts.

15. D.107, 59a.

16. This has been pointed out in Herrmann-Pfandt 2002 and van Schaik 2008a.

17. Lalou 1953, 333–34. The Tibetan titles are (i) *Sgom pa'i rim pa rnam pa gsum,* (ii) *Bsgom pa'i rim pa,* (iii) *Bsgom pa'i rim pa,* (iv) *Byang chub kyi sems sgom pa,* (v) *Byang chub kyi sems sgom pa,* (vi) *Bsgom pa'i sgo bstan,* (vii) *Bsgom pa'i rim pa,* and (viii) *Bsam gtan gi yi ge.* The lists in the *Lhan kar ma* and a later catalog, the *'Phang thang ma,* are also discussed in Faber 1985, 50.

18. This version of the name of the patriarch is similar to the usual form in the Dunhuang manuscripts, which is written *Bo de dar ma ta la,* or just *Dar ma ta la.* This probably represents a transliteration from the Chinese *Damatuolou,* which has been reconstructed by Yanagida (1983, 27–28) as "Dharmatrāta" and by Jeffrey Broughton (1999, 119n5) as "Dharmatāra." I have used the latter name here as it is closer to the Tibetan transliteration.

19. For a description of all of these texts, see van Schaik 2014, 30–34.

20. On the early treasure tradition, see Davidson 2005.

CHAPTER 9: FUNERALS AND MIRACLES

1. Previous studies of Pelliot tibétain 996 include Lalou 1939, Imaeda 1975, and Okimoto 1993.

2. On Artanhwer, see Faber 1985, 73n106; on the location of Anxi, see Beckwith 1987, 197–99.

3. Man Heshang's text, the *Liaoxing ju,* appears in several Dunhuang manuscripts: Pelliot chinois 3434 and 3777, Or.8210/S.3558 and S.4064, and BD08467.

4. Cloud divination text in the Dunhuang manuscript Or.8210/S.3326, translated by Imre Galambos; see the International Dunhuang Project website, idp.bl.uk.

5. On the "rainbow body" (*ja' lus*) in Tibetan Buddhism, see Kapstein 2004; here Kapstein mentions in passing the Chinese contexts of Pelliot tibétain 996.

6. For a selection of the Chinese Amitābha texts, see Giles 1957, 191–92. On the Tibetan Amitābha manuscripts from Dunhuang, see Silk 1993.

7. On the Tibetan presence in Amdo during and after the Tibetan empire, see van Schaik and Galambos 2012. The activities of Gewa Rabsel to suppress the instantaneous teaching are mentioned in *The Religious History of Amdo* (*A mdo'i chos byung*), 223.21. Art-historical evidence for Tibetan Buddhist activities in the area has been discussed in several articles by Amy Heller; see, for example, Heller 1994. On the various sites in the region, see Horleman 2012.

8. Roberto Vitali (1990, 18, 21–22) argues that Man Heshang's patron was Dro Trisumje Tagnang and that he must have been resident in Dunhuang before 810, when, due to a promotion to the rank of minister and general of the northeast army, he would have moved to a major prefecture like Guazhou. There is further evidence in a letter (Pelliot tibétain 1070) written by a Chinese officer to a Zhang Trisumje stating that the latter chose Dunhuang as his residence and founded a temple there. The letter also mentions with respect the father of Zhang Trisumje, suggesting a long-standing association of Dro families with this region. See Demiéville [1952] 2006, 280–90.

9. The Dunhuang copy is a single manuscript split between two collections: IOL Tib J 705 and Pelliot tibétain 818. It has been discussed by Kimura (1981), Okimoto (1993), and van Schaik (2014). On the Tabo and Gondlha versions, see Otokawa 1999 and Tauscher 2007.

10. On the function of manuscript copies of the *Platform Sutra,* see Barrett 2005, 116.

11. The Tibetan translated here as "the path of seeing" is *lam mthong.* This may be equivalent to *mthong lam* (Skt. *darśana-mārga*), the third of the five paths of a bodhisattva, or it may refer to a specific meditation practice.

12. The Tibetan is *rgyal po myes.* It is not clear what reign is referred to here, whether of a specific king or the line of kings of the Yarlung dynasty in general. If the text is referring to the king later known as Myes 'Ag tshom, this is anachronistic, as this ruler, whose official name was Khri lde gtsug btsan, ruled in the first half of the eighth century.

13. The Buddhist narrative of decline mentioned here has been discussed in many places; the best single source is Nattier 1991. The three levels of people mentioned here probably refer to the distinction between inferior, middling, and superior students that appears in

many Buddhist treatises. The distinction is usually invoked less for practical purposes, and more for interpretation of scriptural sources. Here, it seems to be invoked alongside the narrative of decline to justify the use of various methods in teaching, rather than the single method of nonfixation.

14. The above passage seems to be a paraphrase of parts of *Mdo sde brgyad bcu khungs*.

15. This may be the same place as the Yamyog mentioned as the retreat center where Namkai Nyingpo died.

CHAPTER 10: ZEN AND TANTRA

1. This line is in IOL Tib J 508, 19; discussed in van Schaik 2008a, 49.

2. On the overlap between Chinese Chan and tantric practices, see, for example, Tanaka 1981 and Sørensen 1989. On Pelliot chinois 3913, see Tanaka 1981. On this and many other manuscripts concerning maṇḍalas, see Kuo Liying (1998); her investigation of the maṇḍala diagrams of another manuscript, Pelliot chinois 2012, shows how they depart from normative tantric maṇḍalas and how they were used for the three rituals of consecration, confession, and ordination. Though she does not suggest it, the unusual forms of these maṇḍalas and their uses suggest that they also may have been developed in Zen lineages.

3. On critiques of syncretism and recent attempts to rehabilitate the term, see the introduction to Stewart and Shaw 1994.

4. On these manuscripts, see van Schaik and Dalton 2004.

5. On the three concentrations, see van Schaik 2008a.

6. Pelliot tibétain 626, 2v–3r.

7. On Shenxiu's use of metaphor, see McRae 1986. The simile of the thief is also found in the first text in IOL Tib J 710 (translated in chapter 3) and is used by Moheyan in the Chinese version of the *Ratification*, in a quotation of the *Mahāparinirvāṇa sūtra* (Pelliot chinois 4646, 147r–v, translated in Demiéville [1952] 2006, 125).

8. In the translations, the root text is translated directly from the best manuscript version, IOL Tib J 689, with the commentary from Pelliot tibétain 699; thus there are a few minor differences between the translation of the root text and the extracts from it in the commentary.

9. On the *Questions and Answers on Vajrasattva*, see Takahashi 2010. See also the discussion of the Chinese official who copied one version in van Schaik 2008b, 23–26.

10. The interpretation of the colophon here differs from that in van Schaik and Dalton 2004.

11. I have argued elsewhere that the doxographical distinctions made by Nub Sangye Yeshe in the *Lamp for the Eyes of Contemplation* are prescriptive rather than descriptive: see van Schaik 2004b, 2008a. That is, Sangye Yeshe was working to impose the categories of the gradual approach, the instantaneous approach, mahāyoga, and atiyoga and made clear space between each of them. The Dunhuang manuscripts show that such distinctions were of much less significance *in practice* through to the end of the tenth century, almost a hundred years after the composition of the *Lamp*.

12. This quotation is from the *Anantamukhasādhāka-dhāraṇī* (D.914, 249b).

13. My translation here omits the commentary to the first lines of the root text, for reasons of length; the first part of the commentary mainly contains further elaboration on the sufferings of saṃsāra.

14. It has not been possible to identify several of the scriptural citations in the commentary. They may be paraphrases rather than direct quotations.

15. A similar (but not identical) passage is part of the answer to the twenty-eighth question in *Questions and Answers on Vajrasattva* (see translation and edition in Takahashi 2010).

WORKS CITED

This list includes only modern publications. The canonical references for Tibetan and Chinese works mentioned in the text can be found in the endnotes.

Adamek, Wendi. 2007. *The Mystique of Transmission*. New York: Columbia University Press.

———. 2011. *The Teachings of Master Wuzhu: Zen and the Religion of No-Religion*. New York: Columbia University Press.

Anderl, Christoph. 2013. "Was the Platform Sūtra Always a Sūtra?—Studies in the Textual Features of the Platform Scripture Manuscripts from Dùnhuáng." In *Studies in Chinese Manuscripts: From the Warring States Period to the 20th Century*, edited by I. Galambos, 121–76. Budapest: Institute of East Asian Studies, Eötvös Loránd University.

Austin, J. A. (1962) 1971. *How To Do Things with Words*. London: Oxford University Press.

Barrett, T. H. 2005. "Buddhist Precepts in a Lawless World: Some Comments on the Linhuai Ordination Scandal." In *Going Forth: Visions of Buddhist Vinaya*, edited by W. M. Bodiford, 101–23. Honolulu: University of Hawai'i Press.

Beckwith, Christopher. 1987. *The Tibetan Empire in Central Asia*. Princeton: Princeton University Press.

Bretfeld, Sven. 2004. "The 'Great Debate' of bSam yas: Construction and Deconstruction of a Tibetan Buddhist Myth." *Asiatische studien/Études asiatiques* 58, no. 1: 15–56.

Broughton, Jeffrey. 1983. "Early Ch'an Schools in Tibet." In *Studies in Ch'an and Hua-yen*, edited by Robert Gimello and Peter N. Gregory, 1–68. Honolulu: University of Hawai'i Press.

———. 1999. *The Bodhidharma Anthology: The Earliest Records of Zen*. Berkeley: University of California Press.

———. 2009. *Zongmi on Chan*. New York: Columbia University Press.

Cabezón, José. 2001. "Authorship and Literary Production in Classical Buddhist Tibet." In *Changing Minds: Contribution to the Study of Buddhism and Tibet*, edited by Guy Newland, 233–64. Ithaca, N.Y.: Snow Lion Publications.

Cantwell, Cathy, and Robert Mayer. 2013. "Neither the Same nor Different: The Bon *Ka ba Nag po* in Relation to Rnying ma Phur pa Texts." In *Scribes, Texts, and Rituals in Early Tibet and Dunhuang*, edited by Brandon Dotson, Kazushi Iwao, and Tsuguhito Takeuchi, 87–100. Weisbaden: Reichert Verlag.

Cleary, Thomas. 1986. *Zen Dawn: Early Zen Texts from Tun Huang.* Boston: Shambhala Publications.

Cole, Alan. 2009. *Fathering Your Father: The Zen of Fabrication in Tang Buddhism.* Berkeley: University of California Press.

Collins, Randall. 2004. *Interaction Ritual Chains.* Princeton: Princeton University Press.

Culler, Jonathan. 1975. *Structuralist Poetics: Structuralism, Linguistics, and the Study of Literature.* London: Routledge and Kegan Paul.

Dagenais, John. 1994. *The Ethics of Reading in Manuscript Culture.* Princeton: Princeton University Press.

Davidson, Ronald M. 2005. *Tibetan Renaissance: Tantric Buddhism in the Rebirth of Tibetan Culture.* New York: Columbia University Press.

Demiéville, Paul. (1952) 2006. *Le concile de Lhasa: Une controverse sur le quiétisme entre bouddhistes de l'Inde et de la Chine au VIIIe siècle de l'ère chrétienne.* Paris: Institut des hautes études chinoises.

———. 1973. *Choix d'études sinologiques.* Leiden: Brill.

Drikung Kyabgön Chetsang. 2010. *Lanka'i mkhan po dang slob ma'i mdo: Bod rgya shan sbyar* [The record of the Laṅka masters and disciples: Tibetan-Chinese bilingual edition]. Dehradun: Songtsen Library.

Eastman, K. W. 1983. "Mahayoga Texts at Dunhuang." *Bulletin of the Institute of Cultural Studies, Ryukoku University* 22: 42–60.

Faber, Flemming. 1985. "A Tibetan Dunhuang Treatise on Simultaneous Enlightenment: The *Dmyigs Su Myed Pa Tshul Gcig Pa'i Gzhung.*" *Acta Orientalia* 46: 47–77.

Faure, Bernard. 1997. *The Will to Orthodoxy: A Critical Genealogy of Northern Chan Buddhism.* Stanford: Stanford University Press.

Ferguson, Andrew. 2011. *Zen's Chinese Heritage: The Masters and Their Teachings.* Boston: Wisdom Publications.

Gibson, James. 1979. *The Ecological Approach to Visual Perception.* Boston: Houghton Mifflin.

Giles, Lionel. 1957. *Descriptive Catalogue of the Chinese Manuscripts from Tun-huang in the British Museum.* London: British Museum.

Glass, Andrew. 2007. *Four Gāndhārī Saṃyuktāgama Sūtras: Senior Kharoṣṭhī fragment 5.* Seattle: University of Washington Press.

Gnubs sangs rgyas ye shes. 1974. *Rnal 'byor mig gi bsam gtan* [*Lamp for the Eyes of Contemplation*]. Leh, Ladakh: S. W. Tashigangpa.

Gómez, Luis. 1983a. "The Direct and the Gradual Approaches of Zen Master Mahāyāna: Fragments of the Teachings of Mo-ho-yen." In *Studies in Ch'an and Hua-yen,* edited by Robert M. Gimello and Peter N. Gregory, 69–168. Honolulu: University of Hawai'i Press.

———. 1983b. "Indian Materials on the Doctrine of Sudden Enlightenment." In *Early Ch'an in China and Tibet,* edited by Whalen Lai and Lewis Lancaster, 393–434. Berkeley: University of California Press.

Heller, Amy. 1994. "Ninth-Century Buddhist Images Carved at lDan Ma Brag to Commemorate Tibeto-Chinese Negotiations." In *Tibetan Studies: Proceedings of the*

6th International Seminar of the International Association for Tibetan Studies, Fagernes 1992, edited by P. Kværne, 1:335–49. Oslo: Institute for Comparative Research in Human Culture.

Herrmann-Pfandt, Adeleheid. 2002. "The *Lhan kar ma* as a Source for the History of Tantric Buddhism." In *The Many Canons of Tibetan Buddhism,* edited by Helmut Eimer and David Germano, 129–49. Leiden: Brill.

Horleman, Bianca. 2012. "Buddhist Sites in A mdo and Former Long you from the 8th to the 13th Century." In *Old Tibetan Studies: Proceedings of the Tenth Seminar of the IATS, 2003,* edited by Christina Scherrer-Schaub, 119–57. Leiden: Brill.

Imaeda, Yoshiro. 1975. "Documents tibétains de Touen-houang concernant le concile du Tibet." *Journal asiatique* 263: 125–46.

Ingold, Tim. 2000. *The Perception of the Environment: Essays on Livelihood, Dwelling, and Skill.* London: Routledge.

Iwao Kazushi. 2011. "Chibetto shihai shoki no tonkō-shi ni seki suru shin shiryō" [New historical sources on the beginning of the Tibetan control of Dunhuang]. *Dunhuang xieben yanjiū nianbao* 5: 213–24.

Jackson, David. 1994. *Enlightenment by a Single Means: Tibetan Controversies on the Self-Sufficient White Remedy (dKar po Chig thub).* Wien: Verlag der Osterreichische Akademie der Wissenschaften.

Jao, Tsong-yi, and Paul Demièville. 1971. *Airs de Touen-Houang: Textes à chanter des VIIIe–Xe siècles: Manuscrits reproduits en facsimilé.* Paris: Éditions du Centre national de la recherche scientifique.

Jones, A. 2004. "Archaeometry and Materiality: Materials-Based Analysis in Theory and Practice." *Archaeometry* 46, no. 3: 327–38.

Jørgensen, John. 2005. *Inventing Hui-neng, the Sixth Patriarch: Hagiography and Biography in Early Ch'an.* Leiden: Brill.

Kapstein, Matthew. 2000. *The Tibetan Assimilation of Buddhism: Conversion, Contestation, and Memory.* Oxford: Oxford University Press.

———, ed. 2004. *The Presence of Light: Divine Radiance and Religious Experience.* Chicago: University of Chicago Press.

———. 2007. "The Tibetan Yulanpen jing." In *Cultural Contributions to the Cultural History of Early Tibet,* edited by Matthew Kapstein and Brandon Dotson, 211–38. Leiden: Brill.

Karmay, Samten. (1988) 2007. *The Great Perfection (Rdzogs chen).* Leiden: Brill.

Kieschnick, John. 1997. *The Eminent Monk: Buddhist Ideals in Medieval Chinese Hagiography.* Honolulu: Hawai'i University Press.

Kimura, Ryūtoku. 1976. "Tonkō shutsudo chibetto bun shahon Stein 709" [The Dunhuang Tibetan manuscript Stein 709]. *Nihon chibetto gakkai kaihō* 22: 11–13.

———. 1980. "Tonkō chibetto go zen bunken mokuroku shokō" [Tibetan Chan at Dunhuang: A preliminary catalog]. *Tōkyō daigaku bunkabu kōryū shisetsu kenkyū kiyō* 4: 93–129.

———. 1981. "Le dhyāna chinois au Tibet ancien après Mahāyāna." *Journal asiatique* 269: 183–92.

Kuo Liying. 1998. "Maṇḍala et rituel de confession à Dunhuang." *Bulletin de l'Ecole française d'Extrême-Orient* 85: 227–56.

Lalou, Marcelle. 1939. "Document tibétain sur l'expansion du dhyāna chinois." *Journal asiatique* 1939: 505–23.

———. 1953. "Les textes bouddhiques au temps du roi Khri-sroṅ-lde-bcan." *Journal asiatique* 1953: 313–54.

Langer, Rita. 2013. *Sermon Studies and Buddhism: A Case of Sri Lankan Preaching.* Tokyo: International Institute for Buddhist Studies.

Latour, Bruno. 2005. "Thou Shall Not Freeze-Frame—or How Not to Misunderstand the Science and Religion Debate." In *Science, Religion, and the Human Experience,* edited by James D. Proctor, 27–48. Oxford: Oxford University Press.

Liebenthal, Walter. 1953. "The Sermon of Shen-hui." *Asia Major* 3, no. 2: 132–55.

Lin, Pei-Yin. 2011. "Precepts and Lineage in Chan Tradition: Cross-Cultural Perspectives in Ninth-Century East Asia." PhD diss., SOAS, University of London.

Mair, Victor. 1981. "Lay Students and the Making of Written Vernacular Narrative: An Inventory of Tun-huang Manuscripts." *Chinoperl Papers* 10: 5–96.

———. 1983. *Tun-huang Popular Narratives.* Cambridge: Cambridge University Press.

McRae, John. 1986. *The Northern School and the Formation of Early Ch'an Buddhism.* Honolulu: University of Hawai'i Press.

———. 1993. "Yanagida Seizen's Landmark Works on Chinese Ch'an." *Cahiers d'Extrême Asie* 7, no. 7: 51–103.

———. 2003. *Seeing through Zen: Encounter, Transformation, and Genealogy in Chinese Chan Buddhism.* Berkeley: University of California Press.

———. 2005. "Daoxuan's Vision of Jetavana: The Ordination Platform Movement in Medieval Chinese Buddhism." In *Going Forth: Visions of Buddhist Vinaya,* edited by William M. Bodiford, 68–100. Honolulu: University of Hawai'i Press.

Meinert, Carmen. 2006. "Legend of *Cig car ba* Criticism in Tibet: A List of Six *Cig car ba* Titles in the *Chos 'byung me tog snying po* of Nyang Nyi ma 'od zer (Twelfth Century)." In *Tibetan Buddhist Literature and Praxis: Studies in Its Formative Period 900–1400,* edited by Ronald Davidson and Christian Wedemeyer, 31–54. Leiden: Brill.

———. 2007a. "The Conjunction of Chinese Chan and Tibetan rDzogs chen Thought: Reflections on the Tibetan Dunhuang Manuscripts IOL Tib J 689–1 and PT 699." In *Contributions to the Cultural History of Early Tibet,* edited by Matthew T. Kapstein and Brandon Dotson, 239–301. Leiden: Brill.

———. 2007b. "A Pliable Life: Facts and Fiction about the Figure of the Chinese Meditation Master Wolun." *Oriens Extremus* 46: 184–210.

Nanjio Bunyiu. 1923. *The Laṅkāvatāra Sūtra.* Kyoto: Otani University Press.

Nattier, Jan. 1991. *Once Upon a Future Time: Studies in a Buddhist Prophecy of Decline.* Berkeley: Asian Humanities Press.

Norman, Donald. 1988. *The Design of Everyday Things.* London: MIT Press.

O rgyan gling pa. 1983. *Bka' thaṅ sde lṅa* [*The Minister's Edict*]. New Delhi: Jayyed Press.

Obata, Hironobu. 1974. "Chibetto no zhenshū to rekidai hōbōki" [The Tibetan Chan school and the *Lidai fabao ji*]. *Zen bunka kenkyūsho kiyō* 6: 139–76.

Okimoto, Katsumi. 1993. "Daijō mufunbetsu shūjūgi jobun (Pelliot 996) ni tsuite" [Meaning of the practice of nondiscrimination in the Mahāyāna: Concerning Pelliot tibétain 996]. *Hanzano daigaku kenkyū kiyō* 25: 1–23.

Otokawa, Bun'ei. 1999. "New Fragments of the *Rnal 'byor chen por bsgom pa'i don* from Tabo." In *Tabo Studies II,* edited by C. Scherrer-Schaub and E. Steinkellner, 99–161. Rome: Istituto italiano per l'Africa e l'Oriente.

Pachow, Werner. 1979a. "A Study of the Twenty-Two Dialogues on Mahāyāna Buddhism." Part 1. *Chinese Culture, A Quarterly Review* 20, no. 1: 15–64.

———. 1979b. "A Study of the Twenty-Two Dialogues on Mahāyāna Buddhism." Part 2. *Chinese Culture, A Quarterly Review* 20, no. 2: 35–110.

Pasang Wangdu and Hildegarde Diemberger. 2000. *dBa' bzhed: The Royal Narrative concerning the Bringing of the Buddha's Doctrine to Tibet.* Wien: Verlag der Osterreichischen Akademie der Wissenschaften.

Petech, Luciano. 1994. "The Disintegration of the Tibetan Kingdom." In *Tibetan Studies,* edited by Per Kværne, 649–59. Oslo: Institute for Comparative Research in Human Culture.

Poceski, Mario. 2008. "Chan Rituals of Abbots' Ascending the Dharma Hall to Preach." In *Zen Ritual: Studies of Zen Theory in Practice,* edited by Steven Heine and Dale Wright, 83–111. New York: Oxford University Press.

van Schaik, Sam. 2003. "The Great Perfection and the Chinese Monk: rNying-ma-pa Defences of Hwa-shang Mahāyāna in the Eighteenth Century." *Buddhist Studies Review* 20, no. 2: 189–204.

———. 2004a. *Approaching the Great Perfection: Simultaneous and Gradual Approaches to Dzogchen Practice in the Longchen Nyingtig.* Boston: Wisdom Publications.

———. 2004b. "The Early Days of the Great Perfection." *Journal of the International Association of Buddhist Studies* 27, no. 1: 165–206.

———. 2007. "Oral Teachings and Written Texts: Transmission and Transformation in Dunhuang." In *Contributions to the Cultural History of Tibet,* edited by Matthew T. Kapstein and Brandon Dotson, 183–208. Leiden: Brill.

———. 2008a. "A Definition of Mahāyoga: Sources from the Dunhuang Manuscripts." *Tantric Studies* 1: 45–88.

———. 2008b. "The Sweet Saint and the Four Yogas: A 'Lost' Mahāyoga Treatise from Dunhuang." *Journal of the International Association of Tibetan Studies* 4: 1–67.

———. 2013. "Dating Early Tibetan Manuscripts: A Paleographical Method." In *Scribes, Texts, and Rituals in Early Tibet and Dunhuang,* edited by Brandon Dotson, Kazushi Iwao, and Tsuguhito Takeuchi, 119–35. Weisbaden: Reichert Verlag.

———. 2014. *The Tibetan Chan Manuscripts: A Complete Descriptive Catalogue of Tibetan Chan Texts in the Dunhuang Manuscript Collections.* Papers on Central Eurasia 1 (41). Bloomington: Indiana University.

van Schaik, Sam, and Jacob Dalton. 2004. "Where Chan and Tantra Meet: Buddhist

Syncretism in Dunhuang." In *The Silk Road: Trade, Travel, War, and Faith,* edited by
Susan Whitfield, 61–71. London: British Library Press.

van Schaik, Sam, and Imre Galambos. 2012. *Manuscripts and Travellers: The Sino-Tibetan
Documents of a Tenth-Century Buddhist Pilgrim.* Berlin: de Gruyter.

van Schaik, Sam, and Kazushi Iwao. 2008. "Fragments of the Testament of Ba from
Dunhuang." *Journal of the American Oriental Society* 128, no. 3: 477–88.

Schmid, Neil. 2001. "Tun-huang Literature." In *The Columbia History of Chinese Literature,*
edited by Victor Mair, 982–87. New York: Columbia University Press.

Searle, John. 1976. "A Classification of Illocutionary Acts." *Language in Society* 5, no. 1: 1–23.

Seyfort Ruegg, David. 1981. "Autour du lTa ba'i khyad par de Ye shes sde." *Journal asiatique*
269: 207–29.

———. 1992. "On the Historiography and Doxography of the 'Great Debate of bSam yas.'"
In *Tibetan Studies: Proceedings of the 5th Seminar of the International Association for
Tibetan Studies (Narita 1989),* edited by Shoren Ihara, 237–44. Tokyo: Naritisan
Shinshoji.

Shinohara Koichi. 1998. "Evolution of Chan Biographies of Eminent Monks." *Bulletin de
l'Ecole française d'Extrême-Orient* 85: 305–24.

Silk, Jonathan. 1993. "The Virtues of Amitābha: A Tibetan Poem from Dunhuang."
Ryūkoku daigaku bukkyō bunka kenkyūjo kiyō 32: 1–109.

Solonin, Kirill. 2000. "The Tang Heritage of Tangut Buddhism: Teachings Classification in
the Tangut Text 'The Mirror.'" *Manuscripta Orientalia* 6, no. 3: 39–48.

Sørensen, Henrik. 1989. "Observations on the Characteristics of the Chinese Chan
Manuscripts from Dunhuang." *Studies in Central and East Asian Religions* 2: 115–39.

Stearns, Cyrus. 1996. "The Life and Tibetan Legacy of the Indian Mahāpaṇḍita
Vibhūticandra." *Journal of the International Association of Buddhist Studies* 19, no. 1:
127–72.

Stein, R. A. 1983. "Tibetica Antiqua I: Les deux vocabulaires des traductions indo-
tibétaines et sino-tibétaines dans les manuscrits Touen-Houang." *Bulletin de l'École
française d'Extrême-Orient* 72: 149–236.

———. 1984. "Tibetica Antiqua II: L'usage de métaphores pour des distinctions
honorifiques à l'époch des rois tibétaines." *Bulletin de l'École française d'Extrême-
Orient* 73: 257–72.

———. 2010. *Rolf Stein's Tibetica Antiqua, with Additional Materials.* Translated by Arthur
P. McKeown. Leiden: Brill.

Stewart, Charles, and Rosalind Shaw. 1994. *Syncretism/Anti-Syncretism: The Politics of
Religious Synthesis.* London: Routledge.

Takahashi, Kammie. 2010. "Rituals and Philosophical Speculation in the *Rdo rje sems dpa'i
zhus lan.*" In *Esoteric Buddhism at Dunhuang: Rites and Teachings for This Life and
Beyond,* edited by Matthew T. Kapstein and Sam van Schaik, 85–141. Leiden: Brill.

Tanaka, Kenneth, and Raymond Robertson. 1992. "A Ch'an Text from Tun-huang: Impli-
cations for Ch'an Influence on Tibetan Buddhism." In *Tibetan Buddhism: Reason
and Revelation,* edited by S. Goodman and R. Davidson, 57–78. New York: SUNY
Press.

Tanaka Ryōshū. 1981. "Relations between the Buddhist Sects in the T'ang Dynasty through the MS. P. 3913." *Journal asiatique* 269: 163–69.

Tauscher, Helmut. 2007. "The *Rnal 'byor chen po bsgom pa'i don* Manuscript of the 'Gondlha Kanjur.'" In *Text, Image, and Song in Transdisciplinary Dialogue*, edited by D. Klimburg-Salter, K. Tropper, and C. Jahoda, 79–104. Leiden: Brill.

Thomas, F. W., S. Miyamoto, and G. L. M. Clauson. 1929. "A Chinese Mahāyāna Catechism in Tibetan and Chinese Characters." *Journal of the Royal Asiatic Society* 61: 37–76.

Tucci, Guiseppe. (1958) 1978. *Minor Buddhist Texts: Part II.* Rome: Istituto Italiano per il Medio ed Estremo Oriente.

Ueyama Daishun. 1971. "Tonkō shutsudo chibettobun mahaen zenshi ibun" [The lost writings of the Chan master Moheyan]. *Indogaku bukkyōgaku kenkyū* 19, no. 2: 124–26.

———. 1976. "Chibetto yaku tongo shinshū no kenkyū" [A study of the Tibetan translation of the *Dunwu zhenzong yaojue*]. *Zenbunka kenkyūsho kiyō* 8: 33–103.

———. 1982. "Tonkō ni okeru zen no shosō." [Various aspects of Chan Buddhism in Dunhuang]. *Ryūkoku daigaku ronshū* 421: 88–121.

———. 1983. "The Study of Tibetan Ch'an Manuscripts Recovered from Tun-huang: A Review of the Field and Its Prospects." Translated by Kenneth W. Eastman and Kyoko Tokuno. In *Early Ch'an in China and Tibet*, edited by Whalen Lai and Lewis R. Lancaster, 327–50. Berkeley: Asian Humanities Press.

———. 1990. *Tonkō bukkyō no kenkyū* [Studies on Buddhism in Dunhuang]. Kyōto: Hōzōkan.

Vitali, Roberto. 1990. *Early Temples of Central Tibet.* London: Serindia.

Wittgenstein, Ludwig. (1959) 1973. *Philosophical Investigations.* Oxford: Blackwells.

Wright, Dale. 2008. "Introduction: Rethinking Ritual Practice in Zen Buddhism." In *Zen Ritual: Studies of Zen Buddhist Theory in Practice*, edited by Steven Heine and Dale Wright, 3–20. New York: Oxford University Press.

Yamaguchi Zuiho. 1996. "The Fiction of King Dar-ma's Persecution of Buddhism." In *Du Dunhuang au Japon: Études chinoises et bouddhiques offertes à Michel Soymié*, edited by Jean-Pierre Drège, 231–58. Geneva: Droz.

Yampolsky, Philip. 1967. *The Platform Sūtra of the Sixth Patriarch.* New York: Columbia University Press.

———. 1983. "New Japanese Studies in Early Ch'an History." In *Early Ch'an in China and Tibet*, edited by Whalen Lai and Lewis R. Lancaster, 1–12. Berkeley: Asian Humanities Press.

Yanagida Seizan. 1967. *Shoki zenshū shisho no kenkyū* [A study of the historical works of the Zen school]. Kyoto: Hōzōkan.

———. 1974. "Zensekai Kadai." In *Zenke goroku II*, edited by Nishitani Keiji and Yanagida Seizan, 445–514. Tokyo: Chikuma shobō.

———. 1983. "The Li-Tai Fa-Pao Chi and the Ch'an Doctrine of Sudden Awakening." In *Early Ch'an in China and Tibet*, edited by Whalen Lai and Lewis R. Lancaster, 13–50. Berkeley: Asian Humanities Press.

Zieme, Peter. 2012. "The Sūtra of Complete Enlightenment in Old Turkish Buddhism."
    In "Buddhism across Boundaries," edited by John R. McRae and Jan Nattier, *Sino-
    Platonic Papers* 222: 192–211.

INDEX